T0244892

GOD IS OUR HELP

GOD IS OUR HELP

Our Daily Bread Reflections for Living with His Love and Strength

PATRICIA RAYBON

*God Is Our Help: Our Daily Bread Reflections
for Living with His Love and Strength*
© 2024 by Our Daily Bread Publishing

The devotional readings collected in this book were previously published over a span of years in *Our Daily Bread* devotional booklets that are distributed around the world in more than fifty languages.

Requests for permission to quote from this book should be directed to: Permissions Department, Our Daily Bread Publishing, PO Box 3566, Grand Rapids, MI 49501, or contact us by email at permissionsdept@odb.org.

Interior design by Michael J. Williams

ISBN: 978-1-64070-250-9

Library of Congress Cataloging-in-Publication Data Available

Printed in the United States of America
24 25 26 27 28 29 30 31 / 8 7 6 5 4 3 2 1

To Joyce Dinkins, a strong friend, brave editor, and priceless help as we share with joy God's mighty Word

So we say with confidence, "The Lord is my helper;
I will not be afraid."

Hebrews 13:6

CONTENTS

Contents

INTRODUCTION

I wasn't supposed to write these opening words. I'd finished writing *God Is Our Help* when a team member at Our Daily Bread Publishing reminded me to write an introduction to this humble book. I grumbled a bit, to be honest. More writing? Now? But what would I say? In truth, I simply didn't know what to add that would do our mighty God justice and inspire our hopeful hearts.

Then I went to church. Sitting on a pew the next Sunday, I was inspired to hear a soloist lift the weary congregation to our feet. She sang this: "Take your burden to the Lord and leave it there."

The simple song gripped my heart. I grew up hearing the melody in my little childhood church in an earnest part of inner-city Denver. Countless other little churches and singers have sung the beloved song too—many of us not knowing why its unassuming words offer such a powerful witness for a riveting

11

truth: God is real, and when we have a burden, He helps us overcome it. The song's bold words declare it.

> If you trust Him through your doubt,
> He will surely bring you out.
> Take your burden to the Lord and leave
>   it there.

I mention the little song to invite us into these reflections on how God helps us. In countless ways, He helps. So the song's story is worth knowing, and the Lord seemed to invite me to share it. Digging into its background I came upon a child named Charles, born during my nation's slave era—that time of terror and sorrow that I hadn't planned to mention in this collection at all. The era was traumatizing, and its hurts still linger. But here was tiny Charles, born then. And he needed help. We all do.

The little boy Charles, however, had lost both his father, a slave, and his mother, a free woman, by age five. Orphaned and homeless, he sought comfort from his mother's sister, also free, who took Charles in to ensure he too remained free. Yet he wasn't free. Not really.

He couldn't read or write. Hired out as a child to work odd jobs for assorted people, he stayed unschooled for years but remained desperate for learning. Finally, by age seventeen, he'd taught himself the basics of reading. Sitting by firelight every night, he sounded out letters to learn words written on random scraps of paper he'd found.

Still, in young adulthood, after America's Civil War, he could find work only as a hod carrier (brick carrier) and, later, as the unpaid janitor at a Philadelphia church he attended with his new wife, Daisy.

To support them, he toiled long days through his labors. After work hours, he then took night classes and correspondence courses, learning even to read Hebrew and Greek so he could better understand the truth of the Bible. Thus qualified for ordination in the Methodist Episcopal Church, he eventually became pastor of the congregation whose church he'd once cleaned on his hands and knees as a janitor.

Today, Dr. Charles Albert Tindley is remembered as a stunning, stirring preacher and a founding father of gospel music—one who transformed his church of 130 members to a multiracial congregation of 10,000.

How did he overcome his humble beginnings? How do we find help for our setbacks and hardships? To whom do we turn when we don't know where to go?

A core answer is found in the unassuming songs

Tindley wrote about life in God. His roster of nearly fifty hymns includes "Bye and Bye (When the Morning Comes)," "I'll Overcome Someday" (considered the basis for the Civil Rights anthem "We Shall Overcome"), "What Are They Doing in Heaven Today," and "Leave It There."*

He wrote the latter song, according to one story, when a friend came to see him to unload his troubles. After listening to the man's many nagging worries, Tindley told him he needed to take all his troubles, dump them in a sack, then take the sack to God and "leave it there."†

Tindley's homespun advice rings with its biblical basis: "Cast thy burden upon the LORD, and he shall sustain thee" (Psalm 55:22 KJV).

As Jesus declared, "Come to me, all you who are weary and burdened, and I will give you rest" (Matthew 11:28).

---

* "Charles Albert Tindley (1851–1933), Grandfather of Gospel Music," February 18, 2005, Discipleship Ministries, United Methodist Church, https://www.umcdiscipleship.org/resources /charles-albert-tindley-1851-1933-grandfather-of-gospel-music; "Charles Albert Tindley," Hymnary.org, accessed August 29, 2023, https://hymnary.org/person/Tindley_CA.

† Gary Chapman, "Leave It There," A Hymn a Week, Feburary 9, 2013, YouTube video, 5:39, https://www.youtube .com/watch?v=HyxQZQjLaC4.

Above this truth stands our Father God himself—whispering His invitation to remember this:

> Even to your old age and gray hairs
> > I am he, I am he who will sustain
> > > you.
> I have made you and I will carry you;
> > I will sustain you and I will rescue
> > > you.
>
> (Isaiah 46:4)

What does this mean? God is our Help. He was Help to Charles Tindley. He is Help to you and me. So . . .

> Remember the former things, those of
> > long ago;
> > I am God, and there is no other;
> > I am God, and there is none like me.
> > > (v. 9)

May we trust that. Never doubt. He will surely bring us out. Now let's study and praise Him. Hearts on fire. Knowing His help is on its way.

But when?

Right now.

OUR SHELTER IN A TIME OF STORM

It was after ten at night when I headed for home from a club meeting at a new friend's house. To my surprise, when I left, snow was flying. The calendar said *April*, but conditions shouted *blizzard*. Driving on dark, unfamiliar streets, I could barely see the road in front of me. Not even my car lights helped. Reflecting brightly off swirling snow—back into my eyes—the lights barely helped me see a few feet ahead.

Wind-whipped flurries left me feeling disoriented and lost. The closer I got to home, the worse conditions seemed to get. I was surprised to feel panicked. My windshield wipers flew across the glass at top speed. I turned up the car's heater and turned on the window defroster—both barely helping.

Right away, I found myself praying. Praying for help.

But why would God listen? Let alone respond?

These are reasonable questions. Our lives some days can feel storm whipped, disorienting, and downright dangerous.

Will God help? Help as this humble devotional book declares?

He will help—and for one extraordinary reason. God is our Helper—and He loves us.

No, let me say it better. God our Helper loves *me*. Can you look in a mirror and say such life-changing words?

God loves me.

Then, can you believe it?

Seize It

It's *the* concept to grasp to your heart as you read this collection. I state that not as a demand but as a confession: the truth that God loves me has challenged my heart for my entire life. I didn't grow up in a home where love was expressed lavishly. Sure, my hardworking, God-loving, good parents moved mountains for my big sister and me. Thus they got us to our little Black church every Sunday of every month of every year. They made sure we knew Jesus as friend and Savior. They matched us with godly pals, loving teachers, and wholesome activities. They monitored our education—even paying for college when the time came—giving us every opportunity to know more, do more, see more, be more.

But give us a warm hug?

Such needful expression wasn't their way—not their way of giving help. This wasn't their fault. Their generation wasn't shaped, some say, to shower affection as a show of help.

Thus I grew up "hungry for touch" as an expression of help. A healthy touch that affirmed I mattered. Healthy touch that proclaimed I was seen, heard, respected, and understood but was also blessed by helpers who loved me.

What a contrast to popular songs of the day that crooned endlessly about "love." But did the crooning help us know what *love* meant? Did it help me trust the psalmist's announcement that love for me by a helping God "endures"? From "everlasting to everlasting"—even if I could have grasped that idea?

Over and over, however, the writer of Psalm 136 proclaims such a lasting, hard-wearing, warming love. Consider the opening first third of this Bible song:

> Give thanks to the LORD, for he is
> good.

> *His love endures forever.*
> Give thanks to the God of gods.
> *His love endures forever.*
> Give thanks to the Lord of lords:
> *His love endures forever.*
>
> to him who alone does great wonders,
> *His love endures forever.*
> who by his understanding made the
> heavens,
> *His love endures forever.*
> who spread out the earth upon the
> waters,
> *His love endures forever.*
> who made the great lights—
> *His love endures forever.*
> the sun to govern the day,
> *His love endures forever.*
> the moon and stars to govern the night;
> *His love endures forever.*

On and on, this remarkable psalm announces God's love for me—and you—each statement followed by the stunning announcement that God's helping love, for *us*, is both permanent and lavish. Healthy too. Thus it doesn't hold back, shame, condemn, exploit, ridicule, or retreat from us. Thus God's loving help doesn't fade away. Nor grow disinterested. Thus God is never unfaithful. Nor hurtful. Nor does God's great concern or passion for us fade away.

Believe It

The Lord's great help for us, therefore, doesn't get stale. Or turn cold. Or grow intolerant. Or weary when it's past ten o'clock at night, snow is flying, and I can barely see the road beyond a few feet in front of my little car.

God's loving help doesn't fade away.

But there's more. Not even when I have sinned by taking not a snowy road but the wrong road does God stop offering His love that helps.

Many times, answers the writer of Psalm 106, the Lord's rebellious people also "wasted away in their sin" (v. 43), just as you and I have probably sometimes done. And yet?

God "took note of their distress when he heard their cry; . . . and out of his great love he relented," causing "all who held them captive to show them mercy" (see vv. 44–46).

This, then, is the essence of God's help. It's love.

I was confirmed of that in perhaps a strange way. Completing the first novel of a mystery series I've been blessed to write, I allowed a love story to take root in the plot. *But what should my main character's love interest be like?*

Every resource I studied said the "love character" is known most for giving steadying help. Not just a romantic, the love character is committed to being a helper. Committed in the way that God helps us.

Thus, in my snow-whipped car that night, God helped my panic cease. He helped me to see the road so I could drive it wisely and with confidence.

He helped me turn onto the right street and creep my way to the block where my husband and I are blessed to live next to good neighbors who for umpteen years, as my late mother would say, have become beautiful friends

Thus, this same God helped me to write down these plain and humble thoughts in this little reflection as a reminder that "out of his great love for us," He'll never stop helping me, and He'll never stop helping you.

Lavishly. Reliably. Decently. Properly.

On every single day, in fact, His helping love for us is enduring. Ongoing and tolerating, braving and long-suffering, persistent and imperishable—always connecting Him to us. How long? "From everlasting to everlasting" (Psalm 106:48). That's forever and forever.

On even an ordinary day, perhaps like this one, He is ready to help you right this minute because of His durable love. Thus today, right at this minute, ask Him for His loving help.

His answer may be surprising. It may not look like what we expect. It may require us to wait. It may lead us to a story or a Scripture we didn't expect. But because of His great love for us, when we ask Him for help, His answer will be a form of this sweet and loving answer: Sure, my love.

Friendship Bench

*The LORD would speak to Moses face
to face, as one speaks to a friend.*

Exodus 33:11

In the African country of Zimbabwe, war trauma and
high unemployment can leave people in despair—
until they find hope on a "friendship bench." Hopeless
people can go there to talk with trained "grandmoth-
ers"—elderly women taught to listen to people struggling with depression, known in that nation's Shona
language as *kufungisisa*, or "thinking too much."

The Friendship Bench Project is being launched in
other places, including Zanzibar, London, and New
York City. "We were thrilled to bits with the results,"
said one London researcher. A New York counselor
agreed. "Before you know it, you're not on a bench,
you're just inside a warm conversation with someone
who cares."

The project evokes the warmth and wonder of talking with our Almighty God. Moses put up not a bench
but a tent to commune with God, calling it the tent

of meeting. "Inside the Tent of Meeting, the LORD would speak to Moses face to face, as one speaks to a friend" (Exodus 33:11 NLT). Joshua, his assistant, wouldn't even leave the tent, perhaps because he so valued his time with God (v. 11).

Today we no longer need a tent of meeting. Jesus has brought the Father near. As He told His disciples, "Now you are my friends, since I have told you everything the Father told me" (John 15:15 NLT). Yes, our God awaits us. He's our heart's wisest helper, our understanding friend. Talk with Him now.

What worries consume your thoughts today? As you talk to God about these concerns, what good thoughts about Him can you focus on instead?

Dear God, thank you for encouraging our hearts with noble thoughts of you. When we're sick with worry, point our minds back to you, our caring and healing friend.

Exodus 33:9–11 NLT

As he went into the tent, the pillar of cloud would
come down and hover at its entrance while the LORD
spoke with Moses. When the people saw the cloud
standing at the entrance of the tent, they would stand
and bow down in front of their own tents. Inside the
Tent of Meeting, the LORD would speak to Moses
face to face, as one speaks to a friend. Afterward
Moses would return to the camp, but the young man
who assisted him, Joshua son of Nun, would remain
behind in the Tent of Meeting.

A Time to Speak

*There is a time for everything . . . a
time to be silent and a time to speak.*
Ecclesiastes 3:1, 7

For thirty long years, the African American woman worked faithfully for a large global ministry. Yet when she sought to talk with co-workers about racial injustice, she was met with silence. Finally, however, in the spring of 2020—as open discussions about racism expanded around the world—her ministry friends "started having some open dialogue." With mixed feelings and pain, she was grateful discussions began.

Silence can be a virtue in some situations. As King Solomon wrote in the book of Ecclesiastes, "There is a time for everything, and a season for every activity under the heavens: . . . a time to be silent and a time to speak" (3:1, 7).

Silence in the face of bigotry and injustice, however, only enables harm and hurt. Lutheran pastor Martin Niemöller (jailed in Nazi Germany for speaking out) confessed this in a poem he penned after the war.

"First they came for the Communists," he wrote, "but I didn't speak up because I wasn't a Communist." He added, "Then they came for" the Jews, the Catholics, and others, "but I didn't speak up." Finally, "they came for me—and by that time there was no one left to speak up."

It takes courage—and love—to speak up against injustice. Seeking God's help, however, we recognize the time to speak is now.

⁂

Why is it important not to be silent during discussions about injustice? What hinders your willingness to engage in such dialogue?

Dear God, release my tongue and heart from the enemy's grip. Equip me to see and feel the harm of injustice so that I may speak up for those hurt by this sin.

Ecclesiastes 3:1–7

There is a time for everything,
and a season for every activity
under the heavens:

28

a time to be born and a time to die,
a time to plant and a time to
    uproot,
a time to kill and a time to heal,
a time to tear down and a time to
    build,
a time to weep and a time to laugh,
a time to mourn and a time to
    dance,
a time to scatter stones and a time
    to gather them,
a time to embrace and a time to
    refrain from embracing,
a time to search and a time to give
    up,
a time to keep and a time to throw
    away,
a time to tear and a time to mend,
a time to be silent and a time to
    speak.

Asking for Help

"What do you want me to do
for you?" Jesus asked.
Mark 10:51 NLT

Her email arrived late in a long day. In truth, I
didn't open it. I was working overtime to help
a family member manage his serious illness. I didn't
have time, therefore, for social distractions.

The next morning, however, when I clicked on my
friend's message, I saw this question: "Can I help you
in any way?" Feeling embarrassed, I started to answer
no. Then I took a deep breath to pause. I noticed then
that her question sounded familiar—if not divine.

That's because Jesus also asked it. Hearing a blind
beggar call out to Him on the Jericho road, Jesus
stopped to ask this man, named Bartimaeus, a similar
question: Can I help? Or as Jesus said: "What do you
want me to do for you?" (Mark 10:51 NLT).

The question is stunning. It shows that the Healer,
Jesus, longs to help us. But first we're invited to admit
needing Him—a humbling step. The "professional"

beggar Bartimaeus was needy indeed—poor, alone, and possibly hungry and downcast. But wanting a new life, he simply told Jesus his most basic need. "My Rabbi," he said, "I want to see" (v. 51 NLT).

For a blind man, it was an honest plea. Jesus healed him immediately. My friend sought such honesty from me too. So I promised her I'd pray to understand my basic need and, more important, I'd humbly tell her. Do you know your basic need today? When a friend asks, tell it. Then take your plea even higher. Tell God.

〰〰〰〰〰〰〰〰〰〰

"God opposes the proud but shows
favor to the humble." (1 Peter 5:5)

*Lord, I am needy. I want to share my
heart with you now. Help me to humbly
receive the help of others also.*

Mark 10:46–52 NLT

Then they reached Jericho, and as Jesus and his disciples left town, a large crowd followed him. A blind beggar named Bartimaeus (son of Timaeus) was sitting beside the road. When Bartimaeus heard that

Jesus of Nazareth was nearby, he began to shout, "Jesus, Son of David, have mercy on me!"

"Be quiet!" many of the people yelled at him.

But he only shouted louder, "Son of David, have mercy on me!"

When Jesus heard him, he stopped and said, "Tell him to come here."

So they called the blind man. "Cheer up," they said. "Come on, he's calling you!" Bartimaeus threw aside his coat, jumped up, and came to Jesus.

"What do you want me to do for you?" Jesus asked.

"My Rabbi," the blind man said, "I want to see!"

And Jesus said to him, "Go, for your faith has healed you." Instantly the man could see, and he followed Jesus down the road.

His Amazing Help

[God] spreads the snow like wool.

Psalm 147:16

The sheriff marveled at the prayers, estimating "hundreds of thousands or maybe millions of prayers" were lifted to God for help as the East Troublesome Fire raged through the mountains of Colorado in the fall of 2020. Living up to its name, the blaze consumed one hundred thousand acres in twelve hours, roaring through tinder-dry forests, burning three hundred homes to the ground, and threatening entire towns in its path. Then came "the Godsend," as one TV meteorologist called it. No, not rain. A timely snowfall. Arriving early for that time of year, it fell across the fire zone, dropping up to a foot or more of wet snow—slowing the fire and, in some places, stopping it.

Such merciful help seemed too amazing to explain. Does God hear our prayers for snow? And rain too? The Bible records His many answers, including after Elijah's hope for rain (1 Kings 18:41–46). A servant of great faith, Elijah understood God's sovereignty, including over the weather. As Psalm 147 says of God, "He supplies the earth with rain" (v. 8). "He spreads the snow like wool. . . . Who can withstand his icy blast?" (vv. 16–17).

Elijah could hear "the sound of a heavy rain" before clouds even formed (1 Kings 18:41). Is our faith in His power that strong? God invites our trust, no matter His answer. We can look to Him for His amazing help.

꙲꙲꙲꙲꙲꙲꙲꙲꙲꙲꙲꙲

What amazing help have you seen God
bring in a dire situation? How does
His help encourage your faith?

*Amazing God, I bow at your feet, humbled
by your merciful help whenever it comes.
Thank you for encouraging my faith with
your sovereign power throughout the earth.*

Psalm 147:8–17

He covers the sky with clouds;
    he supplies the earth with rain
    and makes grass grow on the hills.

He provides food for the cattle
> and for the young ravens when they
>> call.

His pleasure is not in the strength of
>> the horse,
> nor his delight in the legs of the
>> warrior;
the LORD delights in those who fear him,
> who put their hope in his unfailing
>> love.

Extol the LORD, Jerusalem;
> praise your God, Zion.

He strengthens the bars of your gates
> and blesses your people within you.
He grants peace to your borders
> and satisfies you with the finest of
>> wheat.

He sends his command to the earth;
> his word runs swiftly.
He spreads the snow like wool
> and scatters the frost like ashes.
He hurls down his hail like pebbles.
> Who can withstand his icy blast?

Followed by God's Goodness

Surely your goodness and love will
follow me all the days of my life.

Psalm 23:6

At my first job during my high school years, I worked at a women's clothing store where a security guard dressed as a shopper followed women customers she thought might steal the merchandise. Certain people fit profiles of those the store owners thought were suspicious. Others not considered a threat were left alone. I've been profiled in stores myself and followed, an interesting experience since I still recognize the tactic.

In sharp contrast, David declared he was followed by a divine blessing—God's goodness and mercy. These two gifts always stay close, following him not with suspicion but real love. The "twin guardian angels," as evangelist Charles Spurgeon described the pair, follow believers closely during both bleak days and bright. "The dreary days of winter as well as the bright days of summer. Goodness supplies our needs, and mercy blots out our sins."

As a onetime shepherd, David understood this intentional pairing of goodness and mercy as it's provided by God. Other things could follow believers—fear, worry, temptation, doubts. But "surely," David declares with undoubting certainty, God's kind goodness and loving mercy follow us always.

As David rejoiced, "Surely your goodness and love will follow me all the days of my life, and I will dwell in the house of the LORD forever" (Psalm 23:6). What an amazing gift to follow us home!

How does being followed every day by
God's goodness and love bless your life?
How can you become more aware of God's
goodness and love as they follow you?

*Dear God, thank you for following me
with good intentions and two beautiful
blessings, your goodness and love.*

Psalm 23

The LORD is my shepherd, I lack
      nothing.
  He makes me lie down in green
      pastures,
he leads me beside quiet waters,
    he refreshes my soul.
He guides me along the right paths
    for his name's sake.
Even though I walk
    through the darkest valley,
I will fear no evil,
    for you are with me;
your rod and your staff,
    they comfort me.

You prepare a table before me
    in the presence of my enemies.
You anoint my head with oil;
    my cup overflows.
Surely your goodness and love will fol-
      low me
    all the days of my life,
and I will dwell in the house of the LORD
    forever.

ALL I NEED

Maybe it's one of those days. You know the ones. Not a single thing is going right. Everything you try ends up busted or broken. Out of your mouth fly words you wish you hadn't said. In your head are thoughts you know darn well you shouldn't be thinking. At night, when you're turning and twisting through sleepless hours, your dreams aren't quite nightmares, but they keep you awake because they make no good sense. So when you finally fully open your eyes again, in the gray dawn of another morning, you forget to tell the Lord, *Thank you for delivering my confused soul to a brand-new day.*

Or maybe you've already called friends. You've written in your ink-smeared, overwrought, too-raggedy prayer journal. You've lifted yet another prayer that's so lame and weak it will never reach to that silly popcorn ceiling above your beleaguered head, let alone rise high enough to reach the Lord of Heaven's Armies or the sacred, heavenly home of the Most High.

If that's you today, you can go ahead and declare you're ready to leave that club. I sure am. I've been a member far too long and for countless, too many conflicted, confused reasons.

I even started this devotional book by telling myself—and anybody who'd listen—that I wouldn't have time. I wouldn't know what to say in this devotional collection. I wasn't the right writer. Then out of my mouth came the audacity to ask if the devotional's title couldn't be better. Something fancier? Cooler? Flashier.

God Is Our Help? It lacks star power. Yep, I actually thought that. Are you shaking your head yet? So was I. With eyes only on myself, I fell headfirst into some sort of navel-gazing, self-reliant doubt—about poor me. Poor me, I moaned, isn't good enough. Not famous. Not important. Not right. Not hefty enough to stand in the world behind a too-plain title. *God Is Our Help*?

Was there something snappier?

But God. One night after a dark hour, during one of those infernal sleepless nights, God had the generous kindness to show me what He'd been waiting for me to discover. This little devotional isn't at all about me. So, it's also not at all about you. Not in the end, anyway.

Instead, in the end, it's all about God.

And God—our All—is our Help.

Help when we can't, for the life of us, find help that will actually matter. Help when we've run dirt-dry and can't find one decent drop of water to quench our tough spiritual thirst. Help when nothing else can help because what we need is too enormous and heavy a load for anybody but God.

God is our protection who is always strong—our ever-present help when we're trapped in trouble.

Those relentless sons of Korah put it like this: "God is our refuge and strength, an ever-present help in trouble" (Psalm 46:1).

Those Korah boys got it right. First, *God is*. He's real and ready—yes, God is our protection who is always strong—our ever-present help when we're trapped in trouble.

Maybe nobody in the history of the Bible knew this better than the Korahs' wearied family. Do you recall their story?

Their old man, Korah, was a rebellious, doubting, mean-spirited complainer who, with certain other griping men, challenged the right of Moses and Aaron to the priesthood of God. In response, the Lord opened the earth, letting it swallow Korah along with the other rebels and their households, together with their possessions—never to be seen again (Numbers 16:28–35).

Korah's sons were spared, however, and after seven generations, during David's time, the sons of Korah became famed leaders in choral and orchestral music in the tabernacle. And talk about songwriters. Some eleven psalms in the Bible are credited to the sons of Korah, many noted for gorgeous expressions of pure longing for God, including this beloved verse:

> As the deer pants for streams of water,
>   so my soul pants for you, my God.
> My soul thirsts for God, for the living
>   God.
>   When can I go and meet with God?
>   (Psalm 42:1–2)

Be Still

Talk about beautiful words. Far more astonishing, however, is the clear-eyed confidence they express that, with God as their help, those who profess these truths "will not fear, though the earth give way"—a bold nod, it seems, to the precise thing that marked the end of the psalmists' ancestral father, Korah, who was swallowed up in a fearsome sinkhole.

Here's the whole daring, uncanny, remarkable passage on the power of God's help:

> Therefore we will not fear, though the
> earth give way
> and the mountains fall into the
> heart of the sea,
> though its waters roar and foam
> and the mountains quake with their
> surging.

(Psalm 46:2–3)

I could go on, but the closing refrain of Psalm 46 tells what to do most when we're in a bind.

"Be still, and know that I am God" (v. 10).

The humble reflections of this collection seek to invite us to that daring, holy position—to be still and sink, not into the earth but into the knowing, capable presence of God. When? All the time. Not just when we think there's nothing or no one else who can help, but all the time, God is our help.

43

Hear now the prophet Jeremiah: "Ah, Sovereign LORD, you have made the heavens and the earth by your great power and outstretched arm. Nothing is too hard for you (Jeremiah 32:17).

So, O Lord, will you help?

As we listen, we'll hear His sweet answer: I already have.

In God's Image

God created mankind in his own image,
in the image of God he created them;
male and female he created them.

Genesis 1:27

When her beautiful brown skin started losing its color, a young woman felt frightened, as if she were disappearing or losing her "self." With heavy makeup, she covered up "my spots," as she called them—patches of lighter skin caused by a condition called vitiligo. It's a loss of skin pigment, melanin, which gives skin its tone.

Then one day, she asked herself: Why hide? Relying on God's strength to accept herself, she stopped wearing heavy makeup. Soon she began gaining attention for her self-confidence. Eventually she became the first spokesmodel with vitiligo for a global cosmetics brand.

"It's such a blessing," she told a TV news host, adding that her faith, family, and friends are the ways she finds encouragement.

This woman's story invites us to remember that we

each are created in God's image. "God created human beings in his own image. In the image of God he created them; male and female he created them" (Genesis 1:27 NLT). No matter what we look like on the outside, all of us are image-bearers of God. As His created persons we reflect His glory, and as believers in Jesus we are being transformed to represent Him in the world.

Do you struggle to love the skin you're in? Today, look in the mirror and smile for God. He created you in His image.

〰〰〰〰〰〰〰〰〰〰

What's more important to you—
how people see you or if they see
God in you? What are ways you can
represent God's image to others?

*Help me accept how you've made
me, Creator God. Reign in my heart
so others can see you in me.*

Genesis 1:26–31 NLT

Then God said, "Let us make human beings in our image, to be like us. They will reign over the fish in the sea, the birds in the sky, the livestock, all the wild animals on the earth, and the small animals that scurry along the ground."

> So God created human beings in his
> own image.
> In the image of God he created them;
> male and female he created them.

Then God blessed them and said, "Be fruitful and multiply. Fill the earth and govern it. Reign over the fish in the sea, the birds in the sky, and all the animals that scurry along the ground."

Then God said, "Look! I have given you every seed-bearing plant throughout the earth and all the fruit trees for your food. And I have given every green plant as food for all the wild animals, the birds in the sky, and the small animals that scurry along the ground—everything that has life." And that is what happened.

Then God looked over all he had made, and he saw that it was very good!

Honoring God with Thanks

Call on me when you are in trouble, and I
will rescue you, and you will give me glory.

Psalm 50:15 NLT

The doctor wasn't frowning, despite talking to my husband about a worrying cancer diagnosis. Smiling, she offered a suggestion: start each day by giving thanks. "For at least three things," the doctor said. Dan agreed, knowing that gratitude opens our hearts to find encouragement in God's goodness. Thus, Dan started each day with words of praise. Thank you, God, for a good night's sleep. For my clean bed. For sunshine. For breakfast on the table. For a smile on my lips.

Each word was heartfelt. But could it sound trivial? Does our praise in life's small details matter to Almighty God? In Psalm 50, David's chief musician, Asaph, offers a clear answer. God says, "I do not need the bulls from your barns or the goats from your pens" (v. 9 NLT). Instead of these once-formal Israelite sacrifices of gratitude, God wants us, His

people, to give Him our hearts and lives in gratitude
(vv. 14, 23).

As my husband experienced, whole-hearted gratitude helps our spirits flourish. Then when we call on
the Lord when we are in trouble, He will rescue us
(v. 15). When will He do so? With illness or other
situations, we don't know God's time. But as I write
this now, Dan delights in showing God he's grateful
for His love and for who God is: Redeemer. Healer.
Friend. And friends delight to hear these beautiful
words: Thank you.

<hr/>

What verses bring you comfort in trials?

*My thanks can sound small to me, Lord, so I
thank you for letting my gratitude honor you.*

Psalm 50:8–15 NLT

> I have no complaint about your
>   sacrifices
>   or the burnt offerings you con-
>   stantly offer.

But I do not need the bulls from your
      barns
   or the goats from your pens.
For all the animals of the forest are mine,
   and I own the cattle on a thousand
      hills.
I know every bird on the mountains,
   and all the animals of the field are
      mine.
If I were hungry, I would not tell you,
   for all the world is mine and every-
      thing in it.
Do I eat the meat of bulls?
   Do I drink the blood of goats?
Make thankfulness your sacrifice to
      God,
   and keep the vows you made to the
      Most High.
Then call on me when you are in
      trouble,
   and I will rescue you,
   and you will give me glory.

Surrounded by God

As the mountains surround Jerusalem,
so the Lord surrounds his people
both now and forevermore.

Psalm 125:2

In a busy airport, a young mother struggled alone. Her toddler was in full tantrum mode—screaming, kicking, and refusing to board their plane. Overwhelmed and heavily pregnant, the burdened young mother finally gave up, sinking to the floor in frustration, covering her face, and starting to sob.

Suddenly six or seven women travelers, all strangers, formed a circle around the young mother and her child—sharing snacks, water, gentle hugs, and even a nursery song. Their loving circle calmed the mother and child, who then boarded their plane. The other women returned to their seats, not needing to discuss the help they'd offered, but knowing their support had strengthened a young mother exactly when she needed it.

This illustrates a beautiful truth from Psalm 125:

"As the mountains surround Jerusalem," says verse 2, "so the LORD surrounds his people." The image reminds us how the bustling city of Jerusalem is, indeed, flanked by surrounding hills—among them the Mount of Olives, Mount Zion, and Mount Moriah.

In this same way, God surrounds His people—supporting and standing guard over our souls "both now and forevermore." Thus, on tough days, look up, "unto the hills," as the psalmist puts it (Psalm 121:1 KJV). God awaits with strong help, steady hope, and everlasting love.

How have you sensed the Lord
surrounding you with His love? Whom
can you share His love with today?

*Lord, when we face tough days, surround
our souls with your comforting love.*

Psalm 125:1–5 NLT

Those who trust in the LORD are as
secure as Mount Zion;

they will not be defeated but will
endure forever.
Just as the mountains surround
Jerusalem,
so the LORD surrounds his people,
both now and forever.
The wicked will not rule the land of the
godly,
for then the godly might be tempted
to do wrong.
O LORD, do good to those who are
good,
whose hearts are in tune with you.
But banish those who turn to crooked
ways, O LORD.
Take them away with those who do
evil.

Remember to Sing

How good it is to sing praises to our God.

Psalm 147:1

Nancy Gustafson, a retired opera singer, was devastated when she visited her mother and observed her decline from dementia. Her mom no longer recognized her and barely spoke. After several monthly visits, Nancy had an idea. She started singing to her. Her mother's eyes lit up at the musical sounds, and she began singing too—for twenty minutes! Then Nancy's mom laughed, joking they were "The Gustafson Family Singers." The dramatic turnaround suggested the power of music, as some therapists conclude, to evoke lost memories. Singing "old favorites" has also been shown to boost mood, reduce falls, lessen visits to the emergency room, and decrease the need for sedative drugs.

More research is under way on a music-memory link. Yet, as the Bible reveals, the joy that comes from singing is a gift from God—and it's real. "How good it is to sing praises to our God, how pleasant and fitting to praise him!" (Psalm 147:1).

Throughout the Scriptures, in fact, God's people are urged to lift their voices in songs of praise to Him. "Sing to the LORD, for he has done glorious things" (Isaiah 12:5). "He put a new song in my mouth, a hymn of praise to our God. Many will see and fear the LORD and put their trust in him" (Psalm 40:3). Our singing inspires us and those who hear it as well. May we all remember: our God is great and worthy of praise.

〰〰〰〰〰〰〰〰〰〰

What role does singing play in your life? How can you make more time for singing songs of praise with those who are experiencing memory problems?

May I sing praises to you, God. Thank you for so often unlocking the minds of those with memory problems through the beauty and power of song.

Psalm 147:1–7 NLT

Praise the LORD!

How good to sing praises to our God!
　　How delightful and how fitting!
The LORD is rebuilding Jerusalem
　　and bringing the exiles back to
　　　　Israel.
He heals the brokenhearted
　　and bandages their wounds.
He counts the stars
　　and calls them all by name.
How great is our LORD! His power is
　　　　absolute!
　　His understanding is beyond
　　　　comprehension!
The LORD supports the humble,
　　but he brings the wicked down into
　　　　the dust.

Sing out your thanks to the LORD;
　　sing praises to our God with a harp.

Hope Blossoms

The desert and the parched land will be glad;
the wilderness will rejoice and blossom.

Isaiah 35:1

In the city of Philadelphia, when weedy vacant lots were cleaned up and brightened with beautiful flowers and trees, nearby residents also brightened in overall mental health. This proved especially true for those who struggled economically.

"There's a growing body of evidence that green space can have an impact on mental health," said Dr. Eugenia South, "and that's particularly important for people living in poorer neighborhoods." South, a faculty member at the University of Pennsylvania's Perelman School of Medicine, is coauthor of a study on the subject.

The downtrodden people of Israel and Judah found fresh hope in the prophet Isaiah's vision of their beautiful restoration by God. Amid all the doom and judgment Isaiah foretold, this bright promise took root:

The desert and the parched land will be
glad;

the wilderness will rejoice and
blossom.
Like the crocus, it will burst into bloom;
it will rejoice greatly and shout for
joy.

(Isaiah 35:1–2)

No matter our situation today, we too can rejoice in the beautiful ways our heavenly Father restores us with fresh hope, including through His creation. When we feel down, reflecting on His glory and splendor will bolster us. "Strengthen the feeble hands, steady the knees that give way," Isaiah encouraged (v. 3).

Can a few flowers rekindle our hope? A prophet said yes. So does our hope-giving God.

When you feel hopeless, how do you
usually respond? How could spending
time outdoors in God's creation transform
your despair to renewed hope in God?

*Dear God, thank you for the splendor
of your creation, pointing me to your
glory, and reviving my hope in you.*

Isaiah 35:1–4

The desert and the parched land will be
glad;
    the wilderness will rejoice and
    blossom.
Like the crocus, it will burst into
bloom;
    it will rejoice greatly and shout for
    joy.
The glory of Lebanon will be given to it,
    the splendor of Carmel and Sharon;
they will see the glory of the LORD,
    the splendor of our God.

Strengthen the feeble hands,
    steady the knees that give way;
say to those with fearful hearts,
    "Be strong, do not fear;
your God will come,
    he will come with vengeance;
with divine retribution
    he will come to save you."

NO, NEVER ALONE

In a big city hospital, I saw many hopeful people—but finally I saw my husband. He reached for my hand as I awoke after a frightening surgery. An hour later, when I was wheeled to my hospital room, he again was there waiting for me—his smile assuring me. So I asked my husband to walk with me along the hospital hallway. Walking makes me feel better about things. So despite just having had surgery, I asked Dan to walk with me, and we set off.

All too soon, however, I felt weary. Dan walked me back to my room, where he helped me maneuver into the hospital bed, and then I fell asleep. When I awakened a few hours later, he was still there. And all through the night, every time I woke up—needing help untangling the IV tube so I could turn over, or to call the nurse for something—Dan was there.

Did I look my best? Hardly. In the bathroom mirror, my face had a kind of shocked look to it. My neck was wrapped in bandages. While I was grateful for having access to the medical help I needed, I still felt the physical results of going through it all.

Through it all, however, Dan was there. I suggested he go home and rest. Then he could return later to pick me up for my afternoon departure. But he wouldn't leave. "You might need something," he kept telling me. So he stayed—through it all. A kind, strong, helping, reliable, never-failing, assuring presence and help.

Always with Us

Our Helper God is even more reliable and present in our fragile lives. His words, as recorded by the prophet Isaiah, affirm the true depth of His omnipresent nature. The entire forty-first chapter of Isaiah's proclamations, in fact, declares *who* God is: "Our Helper God." The Help of Israel but also of us. As the Lord declares:

> Do not fear, for I am with you;
>> do not be dismayed, for I am your
>>> God.
> I will strengthen you and help you;

> I will uphold you with my righteous
> > right hand.

> > > (v. 10)

This declaration was made to the children of Israel, who'd spent decades in captivity by the Babylonians but who were finally released when God allowed a pagan king to intervene on their behalf.

It was a dramatic turn of events.

Seeing all this, however, other nations were too stubborn to abandon their idol gods. Instead, in fear, they encouraged each other to make even more idols. As one metalworker said of the welding, "It is good." Another "nails down the idol so it will not topple" (v. 7).

Our God, however, is no metal idol that might fall over if not nailed down in one place. As He said to "my servant" Israel:

> I took you from the ends of the earth,
> > from its farthest corners I called
> > > you.
> I said, 'You are my servant';
> > I have chosen you and have not
> > > rejected you.
> So do not fear, for I am with you;

do not be dismayed, for I am your
God.

(vv. 9–10)

Not held down by distance, time, nor circumstance, the Lord our God is with each of us wherever we find ourselves—sick or well, found or lost, in plenty or in need. Near or far, He is there. I recall praying for a friend facing a medical emergency while she was in Africa on the other side of the globe. But while praying for her, the Lord felt as close as if He *and* she were with me in my humble praying room.

His Detailed Help

In the book of Isaiah, chapter forty-one, our ever-present God describes the exacting nature of His ever-present help.

When others rage against us, opposing us, they "will be as nothing and perish" (v. 11).

If we search for our enemies, "you will not find them. Those who wage war against you will be as nothing at all" (v. 12).

When "the poor and needy search for water, but there is none"—and they're parched with the weary-ing thirst—"I the Lord will answer them; . . . I will make rivers flow on barren heights, and springs within the valleys. I will turn the desert into pools of water, and the parched ground into springs" (vv. 17–18).

When we're spiritually dry and need shade and refreshment, "I will put in the desert the cedar and the acacia, the myrtle and the olive. I will set junipers in the wasteland, the fir and the cypress together" (v. 19).

Why?

"So that people may see and know, may consider and understand, that the hand of the LORD has done this, that the Holy One of Israel has created it" (v. 20).

In truth, in our time, we may think we don't need such lavish help. But the Helper of Israel stands ready to lavishly help us and our loved ones too because He's always with us—seeing and knowing our needs in real time.

The fearful disciples experienced this same reality after Jesus was crucified. Two days later, on the Sunday evening that followed, they gathered behind a locked door "for fear of the Jewish leaders." Still, "Jesus came and stood among them." A locked door, that is, couldn't stop Him from being *there* with them—and there *for* them.

"Peace be with you!" the Lord declared to their anxious hearts (John 20:19).

Then He breathed on them and said, "Receive the Holy Spirit" (v. 22). In a foretaste of the day of Pentecost, the Lord issued to them His spiritual presence—because we need His ever-present guidance and strength to do His work, especially in this tough, often unkind world.

Thus, one week later the Lord Christ was still there for them—and with them. Again the disciples were gathered, this time with their doubting friend Thomas, all still fearful and hiding.

But "though the doors were locked, Jesus came and stood among them" (v. 26).

Are those words sinking into our souls?

Our locked-away lives—along with our fears, burdens, and difficult situations—can't keep God out.

Our locked-away lives—along with our fears, burdens, and difficult situations—can't keep God out. Even in our most dismaying times, He's there—standing among our thorniest foes and even our best of friends.

Telling us what? "Peace be with you!" (v. 26).

As our help, His peace is always and forever

ours—because of who He is. Thomas's response says it all: "My Lord and my God!" (v. 28).

He's the One who is there—because He doesn't abandon us. Not ever. "Take courage! It is I. Don't be afraid," He says (Matthew 14:27), walking across the stormy waves of our lives.

May we praise Him today for such all-the-time love and ever-present help. It's locked into our hearts, and it's always ours. Let's receive Him there.

Sweeter than Honey

Gracious words are a honeycomb, sweet
to the soul and healing to the bones.

Proverbs 16:24

His topic was racial tension. Yet the speaker remained calm and collected. Standing on stage before a large audience, he spoke boldly—but with grace, humility, kindness, and even humor. Soon the tense audience visibly relaxed, laughing along with the speaker about the dilemma they all faced: how to resolve their hot issue but cool down their feelings and words. Yes, how to tackle a sour topic with sweet grace.

King Solomon advised this same approach for all of us: "Gracious words are a honeycomb, sweet to the soul and healing to the bones" (Proverbs 16:24). In this way, "The hearts of the wise make . . . their lips promote instruction" (v. 23).

Why would a powerful king like Solomon devote time to addressing how we speak? Because words can destroy. During Solomon's time, kings relied on messengers for information about their nations, and calm and reliable messengers were highly valued. They used prudent words and reasoned tongues, not overreacting or speaking harshly, no matter the issue.

We all can benefit by gracing our opinions and thoughts with godly and prudent sweetness. In Solomon's words, "To humans belong the plans of the heart, but from the LORD comes the proper answer of the tongue" (v. 1).

⣿⣿⣿⣿⣿⣿⣿⣿⣿⣿

What is your way of speaking when talking about a hot and divisive topic? When you allow God's Spirit to sweeten your tongue, what changes in your words?

Our holy God, when we speak on hard topics, soften our hearts and words with your sweet Spirit.

Proverbs 16:1–2, 21–24

To humans belong the plans of the heart,
but from the LORD comes the
proper answer of the tongue.

69

All a person's ways seem pure to them,
    but motives are weighed by the
        LORD. . . .

The wise in heart are called discerning,
    and gracious words promote
        instruction.

Prudence is a fountain of life to the
        prudent,
    but folly brings punishment to
        fools.

The hearts of the wise make their
        mouths prudent,
    and their lips promote instruction.

Gracious words are a honeycomb,
    sweet to the soul and healing to the
        bones.

Never Give Up

*Keep this Book of the Law
always on your lips.*

Joshua 1:8

"Time went by. War came in." That's how Bishop Semi Nigo of the Keliko people of South Sudan described delays in his church's long struggle to get the Bible in their own language. Not one word, in fact, had ever been printed in the Keliko language. Decades earlier, Bishop Nigo's grandfather had courageously started a Bible translation project, but war and unrest kept halting the effort. Yet despite repeated attacks on their refugee camps in northern Uganda and the Democratic Republic of the Congo, the bishop and fellow believers kept the project alive.

Their persistence paid off. After nearly three decades, the New Testament Bible in Keliko was delivered to the refugees in a rousing celebration. "The motivation of the Keliko is beyond words," said one project consultant.

The commitment of the Keliko reflects the perseverance God asked of Joshua. As God told him, "Keep this Book of the Law always on your lips; meditate on it day and night, so that you may be careful to do everything written in it. Then you will be prosperous and successful" (Joshua 1:8). With equal persistence, the Keliko pursued the translation of Scripture. Now, "when you see them in the camps, they are smiling," said one translator. Hearing and understanding the Bible "gives them hope." Like the Keliko people, may we never give up seeking the power and wisdom of Scripture.

How persistent are you in seeking to read and study Scripture? In what way do you need help in understanding it and who could you ask to help you grow deeper in it?

Loving God, the Bible is vital to my life. Stir up in me a greater hunger to seek, study, and know it, never giving up my quest to understand your wisdom.

Joshua 1:1–9

After the death of Moses the servant of the LORD, the LORD said to Joshua son of Nun, Moses' aide: "Moses my servant is dead. Now then, you and all these people, get ready to cross the Jordan River into the land I am about to give to them—to the Israelites. I will give you every place where you set your foot, as I promised Moses. Your territory will extend from the desert to Lebanon, and from the great river, the Euphrates—all the Hittite country—to the Mediterranean Sea in the west. No one will be able to stand against you all the days of your life. As I was with Moses, so I will be with you; I will never leave you nor forsake you. Be strong and courageous, because you will lead these people to inherit the land I swore to their ancestors to give them.

"Be strong and very courageous. Be careful to obey all the law my servant Moses gave you; do not turn from it to the right or to the left, that you may be successful wherever you go. Keep this Book of the Law always on your lips; meditate on it day and night, so that you may be careful to do everything written in it. Then you will be prosperous and successful. Have I not commanded you? Be strong and courageous. Do not be afraid; do not be discouraged, for the LORD your God will be with you wherever you go."

A Big Deal

This is the kind of fasting I want: . . .
Let the oppressed go free, and remove
the chains that bind people.

Isaiah 58:6 NLT

A family member needed help with his December rent. To his family the request felt like a burden, especially with their own unexpected expenses at year's end. But they dug into their savings, grateful for God's provision and blessed by their relative's gratitude. He handed them a thank-you card filled with grateful words. "There you go again . . . doing nice things, probably passing it off as no big deal."

Helping others is a big deal, however, to God. The prophet Isaiah made that point to the nation of Israel. The people were fasting but still quarreling and fighting. Instead, said God through Isaiah,

> Free those who are wrongly
> imprisoned;
> lighten the burden of those who
> work for you. . . .

Share your food with the hungry,
and give shelter to the homeless.
Give clothes to those who need them,
and do not hide from relatives who
need your help.
(Isaiah 58:6–7 NLT)

Such a sacrifice, said Isaiah, shares God's light but also heals our own brokenness (v. 8).

As the family helped their relative, they looked hard at their own finances, seeing ways they could manage better all year. This was God's promise for being generous: "Your godliness will lead you forward, and the glory of the LORD will protect you from behind" (v. 8 NLT). In the end, giving to their kin blessed them more. And God? He already gave His all—with love.

God gave His all. Will we
follow where He leads?

Lord, light the path of generosity,
helping us to give like you.

Isaiah 58:6–9 NLT

This is the kind of fasting I want:
Free those who are wrongly imprisoned;
> lighten the burden of those who
> > work for you.
Let the oppressed go free,
> and remove the chains that bind
> > people.
Share your food with the hungry,
> and give shelter to the homeless.
Give clothes to those who need them,
> and do not hide from relatives who
> > need your help.

Then your salvation will come like the
> > dawn,
> and your wounds will quickly heal.
Your godliness will lead you forward,
> and the glory of the LORD will pro-
> > tect you from behind.

Then when you call, the LORD will
> > answer.
> "Yes, I am here," he will quickly
> > reply.

Remove the heavy yoke of oppression.
Stop pointing your finger and
spreading vicious rumors!

Expect the Messiah

Isn't this the carpenter's son? Isn't his mother's name Mary?

Matthew 13:55

The repairman looked young—too young to fix our problem, an old car that wouldn't start. "He's just a kid," my husband, Dan, whispered to me, showing his doubt. His disbelief in the young man sounded like the grumbling in Nazareth, where citizens doubted who Jesus was.

"Isn't this the carpenter's son?" they scoffed when Jesus taught in the synagogue (Matthew 13:55). They were surprised that someone they knew was healing and teaching. "Where did this man get this wisdom and these miraculous powers?" (v. 54). Instead of trusting in Jesus, they were offended by the authority he displayed (vv. 15, 58).

In this same way, we may struggle to trust in our Savior's wisdom and power, especially in the familiar and ordinary details of our daily lives. Failing to expect His help, we may miss out on the wonder of His life transforming our own (v. 58).

As Dan found, the help he needed stood right in front of him. Finally agreeing to accept the young man's aid, my husband allowed him to look at our car's battery. By switching just one bolt, the mechanic had the car running in seconds—engine humming and lights ablaze. "It lit up like Christmas," Dan said.

So too may we expect and experience the Messiah bringing fresh light, life, and help into our daily journey with Him.

What are some practical ways you
can remind yourself or others that
God is in control and He is able?

When I doubt you, Lord, help my unbelief.

Matthew 13:53–58

When Jesus had finished these parables, he moved on from there. Coming to his hometown, he began teaching the people in their synagogue, and they were amazed. "Where did this man get this wisdom and these miraculous powers?" they asked. "Isn't this the carpenter's son? Isn't his mother's name Mary, and aren't his brothers James, Joseph, Simon and Judas? Aren't all his sisters with us? Where then did this man get all these things?" And they took offense at him.

But Jesus said to them, "A prophet is not without honor except in his own town and in his own home."

And he did not do many miracles there because of their lack of faith.

Simply Ask

Before they call I will answer.
Isaiah 65:24

Her doctor said her detached retinas couldn't be repaired. But after living without sight for fifteen years—learning Braille and using a cane and service dog—a Montana woman's life changed when her husband asked another eye doctor a simple question: Could she be helped? The answer was yes. As the doctor discovered, the woman had a common eye condition, cataracts, which the doctor removed from her right eye. When the eye patch came off the next day, her vision was 20/20. A second surgery for her left eye met with equal success.

A simple question also changed the life of Naaman, a powerful military man with leprosy. Naaman had raged arrogantly at the prophet Elisha's instructions to "wash yourself seven times in the Jordan, and your flesh will be restored" (2 Kings 5:10). Naaman's servants, however, asked the military leader a simple question: "If the prophet had told you to do some great thing, would you not have done it?" (v. 13). Persuaded, Naaman washed, "and his flesh was restored and became clean" (v. 14).

In our lives, sometimes we struggle with a problem because we won't ask God. Will you help? Should I go? Will you lead? He doesn't require complicated questions from us to help. "Before they call I will answer," God promised His people (Isaiah 65:24). So today, simply ask Him.

〰〰〰〰〰〰〰〰〰〰

How complex are your prayer requests? What life problem can you offer to God in a simple prayer?

Dear heavenly Father, when life feels complicated and difficult, thank you for your promise to hear even our simple prayers.

2 Kings 5:9–14

Naaman went with his horses and chariots and stopped at the door of Elisha's house. Elisha sent a messenger to say to him, "Go, wash yourself seven times in the Jordan, and your flesh will be restored and you will be cleansed."

But Naaman went away angry and said, "I thought that he would surely come out to me and stand and call on the name of the LORD his God, wave his hand over the spot and cure me of my leprosy. Are not Abana and Pharpar, the rivers of Damascus, better than all the waters of Israel? Couldn't I wash in them and be cleansed?" So he turned and went off in a rage.

Naaman's servants went to him and said, "My father, if the prophet had told you to do some great thing, would you not have done it? How much more, then, when he tells you, 'Wash and be cleansed'!" So he went down and dipped himself in the Jordan seven times, as the man of God had told him, and his flesh was restored and became clean like that of a young boy.

WHAT A FRIEND

The freed man described with one word the twenty-eight years he'd spent in prison for a murder he said he didn't commit. He felt *heavy*. That's how the ordeal felt—a burden of wrongful imprisonment that felt too weighty for him alone to move.

Then he found a friend.

Retired teacher Ginny had started writing Lamar weekly letters. For nearly all of the twenty-eight years Lamar was behind bars in Missouri, Ginny penned encouragement, faith, and uplifting hope—sharing her own struggles, lifting Lamar's load by telling him hers and listening to his.

Their friendship was an unlikely one, to be sure. After Lamar's 1994 conviction in the murder of his best friend, he'd felt so lonely and lost he started writing letters to churches, "seeking somebody who could give me support and friendship," he explained in a newspaper article.

One letter ended up with Ginny. A member of a St. Louis church, she was asked by a deacon to find someone to reply to a letter from a prison inmate. Ginny decided to write to Lamar herself.

Opening his letter, she was "blown away" first by Lamar's impressive handwriting. "His cursive just put me to shame," she told a newspaper reporter.* His language skills conveyed a bright intelligence, all of it locked away behind bars in a man who insisted he hadn't killed anybody.

Then, finally and slowly, breaks in his case occurred. First, in both 1996 and 2002, another man confessed to the crime, saying Lamar wasn't involved. But Lamar lost several appeals in state and federal courts. Another break came in 2019 when a report documented that police and prosecutors falsified evidence in Lamar's case. As well, the St. Louis Circuit Attorney's Office secretly paid its only eyewitness, the report confirmed, to identify Lamar as the shooter.

Still, Lamar remained in prison another four long

---

* Sydney Page, "Exonerated Man, Freed after 28 Years, Reunites with Pen Pal Who Wrote Him Weekly" *Washington Post*, April 28, 2023, https://www.washingtonpost.com/lifestyle/2023/04/28/exonerated-man-freed-after-28-years-reunites-with-pen-pal-who-wrote-him-weekly/.

years—unable alone to lift the weight of a conviction that seemed immovable. Then finally, at age forty-nine—after intervention by the Innocence Project along with the strength of Ginny's unwavering friendship—Lamar was freed when a Missouri judge overturned Lamar's first-degree murder conviction.

Breakthrough Help

How, then, did Lamar feel? *Lighter*. "It felt like 28 years of weight was slowly being lifted."

The psalmist described such a moment like this:

> I was pushed back and about to fall,
>   but the LORD helped me.
> The LORD is my strength and my
>   defense;
>   he has become my salvation.
>   (Psalm 118:13–14)

Both that psalm and Lamar's story bring to mind the great weight that only God could lift from the Israelites. Weighed down, they'd suffered under enslavement by the Egyptians for four hundred years.

Then, with power, God defeated Pharaoh's army as they pursued God's people by chariot into the Red Sea. As God threw their forces into confusion and their chariots' wheels into useless, twisted disrepair, the Egyptians cried in terror. "Let's get out of here—away from these Israelites!" Indeed, "the LORD is fighting for them against Egypt" (Exodus 14:25 NLT).

May we not overlook, however, how the freed Israelites responded to their delivering God. Along with Moses, they sang a song—lifting their voices to God with thanksgiving and joy about *His strength*. "The LORD is my strength and my song; he has given me victory" (15:2 NLT). This people who'd felt *without* strength for generations, who'd known only weakness as they toiled under the merciless oppression of a heavy-handed enemy, now sang of the strong, helping might of their invincible, delivering God.

"Your right hand, O LORD, is glorious in power. Your right hand, O LORD, smashes the enemy" (v. 6 NLT). Their song went on:

> In the greatness of your majesty,
> you overthrow those who rise
> against you. . . .
>
> The enemy boasted,
> "I will chase them and catch up
> with them.

> I will plunder them
>> and consume them." . . .
> But you blew with your breath,
>> and the sea covered them.
> They sank like lead
>> in the mighty waters.
>
> (vv. 7, 9–10 NLT)

Not content to stop there, the Israelites continued singing about God's incomparable strength: "The power of your arm," sang the Israelites about God, "makes [our enemies] lifeless as stone until your people pass by, O LORD" (v. 16 NLT).

As an inmate, Lamar would attest that it takes a strong defense to defeat a relentless, unyielding foe.

Helping Strength

But God is our strength—and that is a significant way He helps us.

"He remembered us in our weakness," wrote the psalmist in Psalm 136:23 (NLT). Knowing that we are often weak—physically and spiritually—He steps in with the spiritual might we need to power through what looks impossible to move.

But what else is remarkable?

God will send His help to us through other people—providing it even if we don't know when or how.

God will send His help to us through other people—providing it even if we don't know when or how.

Lamar experienced such help through Ginny's faithful weekly letters. Thus he could "lean on her and express how I was feeling about my situation."*

In the same way, God invites us to lean on Him when we need His strong right hand to hold us up. As He told the children of Israel:

"Don't be afraid, for I am with you. Don't be discouraged, for I am your God. I will strengthen you and help you. I will hold you up with my victorious right hand." (Isaiah 41:10 NLT)

Glory, indeed, to His name:

"For I hold you by your right hand—I, the LORD your God. And I say to you, 'Don't be afraid. I am here to help you.'" (v. 13 NLT)

* Sydney Page, "Exonerated man."

Does it get any clearer for us than that? That God's great strength lifts us above our burdens. Lamar isn't even angry about the twenty-eight years he lost to prison. Instead, he is "focused on making up for lost time and enjoying his life," a newspaper writer reported.

Such deliverance comes only from God—our Strong Deliverer. He longs to help us with strength today. May we come to Him and lean, letting His strength hold us up in all our weak places.

"For when I am weak," said the apostle Paul, then in God's strength "I am strong" (2 Corinthians 12:10). Paul even prayed this for us in Christ: "that out of his glorious riches he may strengthen you with power through his Spirit in your inner being" (Ephesians 3:16).

May God answer that prayer right now, breaking chains—for you and for me.

Then, before they even fall, let us shout *amen*.

Brave Your Storm

*[Fix your] eyes on Jesus, . . . so that you
will not grow weary and lose heart.*

Hebrews 12:2–3

It was the evening of April 3, 1968, and a fierce
thunderstorm was lashing through Memphis, Ten-
nessee. Weary and feeling ill, the Rev. Dr. Martin
Luther King Jr. decided to cancel his planned speech
in support of the striking sanitation workers at a
church hall. But he was surprised by an urgent phone
call saying a large crowd had braved the weather to
hear him. So he went to the hall and spoke for forty
minutes, delivering what some say was his greatest
speech, "I've Been to the Mountaintop."

The next day, King was killed by an assassin's bullet,
but his speech still inspires oppressed people with the
hope of "the promised land." Likewise, early followers of Jesus were uplifted by a stirring message. The
book of Hebrews, written to encourage Jewish believers facing threats for their faith in Christ, offers firm
spiritual encouragement to not lose hope. As it urges,

"strengthen your feeble arms and weak knees" (12:12). As Jews, they would recognize that appeal as originally coming from the prophet Isaiah (Isaiah 35:3).

But now, as Christ's disciples, we're called to "run with perseverance the race marked out for us, fixing our eyes on Jesus, the pioneer and perfecter of faith" (Hebrews 12:1–2). When we do so, we "will not grow weary and lose heart" (v. 3).

Certainly, squalls and storms await us in this life. But in Jesus, we outlast life's tempests by standing strong in Him.

<hr />

How do you respond to life's spiritual storms? As you look to Jesus and His promises, how does He encourage you?

Jesus, you calm every spiritual storm.
When tempests rage, speak peace to
my soul as I put my hope in you.

Hebrews 12:1–3, 12–13

Therefore, since we are surrounded by such a great cloud of witnesses, let us throw off everything that hinders and the sin that so easily entangles. And let us run with perseverance the race marked out for us, fixing our eyes on Jesus, the pioneer and perfecter of faith. For the joy set before him he endured the cross, scorning its shame, and sat down at the right hand of the throne of God. Consider him who endured such opposition from sinners, so that you will not grow weary and lose heart. . . .

Therefore, strengthen your feeble arms and weak knees. "Make level paths for your feet," so that the lame may not be disabled, but rather healed.

Never Late

Your brother will rise again.

John 11:23

As a visitor to a small West African town, my American pastor made sure to arrive on time for a 10:00 a.m. Sunday service. Inside the humble sanctuary, however, he found the room empty. So he waited. One hour. Two hours. Finally, about 12:30 p.m., when the local pastor arrived after his long walk there, followed by some choir members and a gathering of friendly town people, the service began—"in the fullness of time," as my pastor said. "The Spirit welcomed us, and God wasn't late." My pastor understood the culture was different there for its own good reasons.

Time can seem relative, but God's perfect on-time nature is affirmed throughout the Scriptures. Thus, after Lazarus got sick and died, Jesus arrived four days later, with Lazarus's sisters asking why. "'Lord,' Martha said to Jesus, 'if you had been here, my brother would not have died'" (John 11:21). We may think the same, wondering why God doesn't hurry to fix our problems now. Better instead to wait by faith for His answers and power.

As theologian Howard Thurman wrote, "We wait, our Father, until at last something of thy strength becomes our strength, something of thy heart becomes our heart, something of thy forgiveness becomes our forgiveness. We wait, O God, we wait." Then, as with Lazarus, when the Lord responds, we're miraculously blessed by what wasn't, after all, a delay.

What are you waiting for God
to do or provide on your behalf?
How can you wait by faith?

For you, O Lord, we wait. Grant us your strength and faithful hope in our waiting.

John 11:17–34

On his arrival, Jesus found that Lazarus had already been in the tomb for four days. Now Bethany was less than two miles from Jerusalem, and many Jews had come to Martha and Mary to comfort them in the loss of their brother. When Martha heard that Jesus was coming, she went out to meet him, but Mary stayed at home.

"Lord," Martha said to Jesus, "if you had been here, my brother would not have died. But I know that even now God will give you whatever you ask."

Jesus said to her, "Your brother will rise again."

Martha answered, "I know he will rise again in the resurrection at the last day."

Jesus said to her, "I am the resurrection and the life. The one who believes in me will live, even though they die; and whoever lives by believing in me will never die. Do you believe this?"

"Yes, Lord," she replied, "I believe that you are the Messiah, the Son of God, who is to come into the world."

After she had said this, she went back and called her sister Mary aside. "The Teacher is here," she said, "and is asking for you." When Mary heard this, she got up quickly and went to him. Now Jesus had not yet entered the village, but was still at the place where Martha had met him. When the Jews who had been with Mary in the house, comforting her, noticed how quickly she got up and went out, they followed her, supposing she was going to the tomb to mourn there.

When Mary reached the place where Jesus was and saw him, she fell at his feet and said, "Lord, if you had been here, my brother would not have died."

When Jesus saw her weeping, and the Jews who had come along with her also weeping, he was deeply moved in spirit and troubled. "Where have you laid him?" he asked.

Loving the Stranger

Do not mistreat or oppress a foreigner,
for you were foreigners in Egypt.

Exodus 22:21

After a member of my family converted to a different religion, Christian friends urged me to "convince" her to return to Jesus. I found myself first seeking to love my family member as Christ would—including in public places where some people frowned at her "foreign-looking" scarves and clothes. Others even made rude comments. "Go home!" one man yelled at her from his truck, not knowing or apparently caring that she already was "home."

Moses taught a much kinder way to act toward people whose dress or beliefs are different. Teaching laws of justice and mercy, Moses instructed the children of Israel, "Do not oppress a foreigner; you yourselves know how it feels to be foreigners, because you were foreigners in Egypt" (Exodus 23:9). The edict expresses God's concern for all strangers, people vulnerable to bias and abuse, and it is repeated in Exodus 22:21 and Leviticus 19:33.

Therefore, when I spend time with my family member—at a restaurant, in a park, taking a walk together or sitting and talking with her on my front porch—I seek first to show her the same kindness and respect that I would want to experience. It's one of the best ways to remind her of the sweet love of Jesus, not by shaming her for rejecting Him but by loving her as He loves all of us—with amazing grace.

What attitudes do you hold about people who appear "different" or "foreign"? In what ways can you practice God's edict to not mistreat a "stranger" or "sojourner" in your land?

Gracious Father, open my heart today to a stranger or foreigner in my land, helping them to encounter you.

Exodus 23:1–9

Do not spread false reports. Do not help a guilty person by being a malicious witness.

Do not follow the crowd in doing wrong. When you give testimony in a lawsuit, do not pervert justice by siding with the crowd, and do not show favoritism to a poor person in a lawsuit.

If you come across your enemy's ox or donkey wandering off, be sure to return it. If you see the donkey of someone who hates you fallen down under its load, do not leave it there; be sure you help them with it.

Do not deny justice to your poor people in their lawsuits. Have nothing to do with a false charge and do not put an innocent or honest person to death, for I will not acquit the guilty.

Do not accept a bribe, for a bribe blinds those who see and twists the words of the innocent.

Do not oppress a foreigner; you yourselves know how it feels to be foreigners, because you were foreigners in Egypt.

Watched by God

The LORD watches over you.
Psalm 121:5

Our little grandson waved goodbye, then turned back with a question. "Grandma, why do you stand on the porch and watch until we leave?" I smiled at him, finding his question "cute" because he was so young. Seeing his concern, however, I tried to give a good answer. "Well, it's a courtesy," I told him. "If you're my guest, watching until you leave shows I care." He weighed my answer but still looked perplexed. So I told him the simple truth. "I watch," I said, "because I love you. When I see your car drive away, I know you're safely heading home." He smiled, giving me a tender hug. Finally he understood.

His childlike understanding reminded me what all of us should remember—that our heavenly Father is constantly watching over each of us, His precious children. As Psalm 121 says, "The LORD watches over you—the LORD is your shade at your right hand" (v. 5).

What assurance for Israel's pilgrims as they climbed dangerous roads to Jerusalem to worship. "The sun will not harm you by day, nor the moon at night. The LORD will keep you from all harm—he will watch over your life" (vv. 6–7). Likewise, as we each climb our life's road, sometimes facing spiritual threat or harm, "The LORD will watch over [our] coming and going." Why? His love. When? "Now and forevermore" (v. 8).

※※※※※※※※※※※※※※

What "mountain" are you climbing today? What assurance do you find in knowing God is watching over you?

Our loving Father, as we travel the road of life, thank you for watching over us, keeping us safe.

Psalm 121:5–8

The LORD watches over you—
the LORD is your shade at your
right hand;
the sun will not harm you by day,
nor the moon by night.

The LORD will keep you from all
      harm—
  he will watch over your life;
the LORD will watch over your coming
     and going
  both now and forevermore.

Fruit Juice

A thrift-store bargain, the lamp seemed perfect for my home office—the right color, size, and price. Back at home, however, when I plugged in the cord, nothing happened. No light. No power. No juice.

No problem, my husband assured me. "I can fix that. Easy." As he took the lamp apart, he saw the trouble immediately. The plug wasn't connected to anything. Without wiring to a source of power, the "perfect" pretty lamp was useless.

The same is true for us. Jesus told His disciples, "I am the vine; you are the branches. If you remain in me and I in you, you will bear much fruit." But then he added this reminder: "Apart from me you can do nothing" (John 15:5).

This teaching was given in a grape-growing region, so His disciples readily understood it. Grapevines are hardy plants, and their branches tolerate vigorous pruning. Cut off from their life source, however, the branches are worthless deadwood. So it is with us.

As we remain in Jesus and let His words dwell in us, we're wired to our life source—Christ himself. "This is to my Father's glory," said Jesus, "that you bear much fruit, showing yourselves to be my disciples" (v. 8). Such a fruitful outcome needs daily nourishment, however. Freely, God provides it through the Scriptures and His love. So plug in and let the juice flow!

What does it mean for you to remain
in Jesus? How has He equipped
you to bear fruit for Him?

*All-powerful God, empower me to
remain in you and allow your loving
Word to yield good fruit in me.*

John 15:5–8

I am the vine; you are the branches. If you remain in me and I in you, you will bear much fruit; apart from me you can do nothing. If you do not remain in me, you are like a branch that is thrown away and withers; such branches are picked up, thrown into the fire and burned. If you remain in me and my words remain in you, ask whatever you wish, and it will be done for you. This is to my Father's glory, that you bear much fruit, showing yourselves to be my disciples.

NOBODY GREATER

We're at a spring wedding, and everything is glorious. The bride is beautiful, smiling, and glowing. The groom is handsome, proud, and beaming. We've known the bride since she was in preschool, so we feel joyous to watch her—as a professional young woman now—escorted by her dad down a long, winding staircase toward her groom.

To set the tone, the steps are flanked by beautiful floral arrangements—a stunning accompaniment to the bride's lovely wedding gown. Later, in a reception hall lined with floor-to-ceiling windows, bursts of fireworks from another celebration nearby seem to give this wedding's festivities an extra spark of glee.

The day feels close to perfect, in fact, in so many lovely and also holy ways. As friends and parents remark during the wedding toasts, "Remember to put God first and you'll remain on the right path."

As obvious as it seems to say it, God Almighty

seemed to have blessed that celebration. The mother of the bride declared so herself when she and I huddled in a quiet moment during the reception to chat about the beautiful day. "God is so good," she stated, showing gratitude.

"So good indeed," I agreed.

Always Good?

But what about on ordinary days? Or awful ones?

What if a wedding isn't glorious? Or gloomy clouds drip stormy rain? Or a sorrowing disappointment is overwhelming my mortal life? Or yours?

Do we need more examples? Just watch the news on any average day. The ripple of horror and heartbreak is enough to make the most fervent believer confront moments of doubt. The evil that people do can be beyond reckoning.

I could recount here some of the worst examples, including wars and rumors of wars and beyond. But we already each know—sometimes personally—of human evil or physical failure or emotional terror that seizes the heart and mind, making life feel impossible to bear. In the pit of such despair, many can't find the wherewithal to leap from that pit to shout with joy and certainty that God is good.

But that doesn't change the irrefutable truth that God *is* good. Always good. How? His very nature is good. As Jesus proclaimed, "No one is good—except God alone" (Luke 18:19). As theologians declare, God can't act in any way outside of that nature.

Scripture rings out, therefore, with declarations of God's goodness. As the psalmist David wrote:

> Do not remember the sins of my youth
>   and my rebellious ways;
> according to your love remember me,
>   for you, LORD, are good.
>
> Good and upright is the LORD.
>   (Psalm 25:7–8)

Likewise, James speaks with perfect trust in the essential nature of God's being as goodness. "Every good and perfect gift is from above, coming down from the Father of the heavenly lights, who does not change like shifting shadows" (James 1:17).

How, then, can we cling to the Lord's unchanging goodness, especially in the face of the world's evil? We cling because we know this of evil: God didn't create it.

Instead, evil is the absence of goodness. Thus, wherever evil is, God isn't. Not even God's wrath is evil.

God's wrath is just. Unlike human wrath, which usually is tainted with anger, God's wrath is formed by God's righteousness. Thus, "vengeance is mine," the Lord says—reminding us with clarity to back away from human acts of reprisal (Deuteronomy 32:35; Romans 12:19 ESV).

This important distinction cautions us mortals to never assume the role of God in exacting punishment on one another. We'll get it wrong when we do.

> **From sea to shining sea, God's goodness can be seen, felt, heard, marveled over in every moment of every hour.**

The Goodness in Him

In stark contrast, from the beginning of biblical time, "God saw all that he had made, and it was very good" (Genesis 1:31).

Thus we see God's goodness in His creation. In the rising sun of a new day. A glowing sunset as evening closes. In the busy chirp of garden birds. In the stunning petals of gorgeous flowers. In a starry night. In the waves of rivers, streams, and oceans. From sea to shining sea, God's goodness can be seen, felt, heard, marveled over in every moment of every hour—in His creation, yes.

So it's no surprise that the prophet Jeremiah declared that truth this way: "Ah, Sovereign LORD, you have made the heavens and the earth by your great power and outstretched arm. Nothing is too hard for you" (Jeremiah 32:17).

As David too beheld God's creation, he also avowed: "The heavens declare the glory of God; the skies proclaim the work of his hands (Psalm 19:1). As for the sun, "it rises at one end of the heavens and makes its circuit to the other; nothing is deprived of its warmth." Therefore, writes David, "The law of the LORD is perfect, refreshing the soul" (vv. 6–7).

We also see God's goodness in His Word. When we need help, therefore, we can find it recorded in the book of His goodness—in His Holy Bible.

"The LORD is good to all," wrote David. "He has compassion on all he has made" (145:9). The record of God's goodness is set down to confirm His goodness, from first page to final page.

In these ways, we can trust Him, therefore, to help us—in His goodness—because good is who He is and what God does.

At that spring wedding, when the weather suddenly

turned cold and the unseasonable weather could've put a damper on the festivities, the atmosphere grew cozy, warm, and even fun as wedding guests—and the bride and groom—pulled closer to one another.

God in His goodness also gave guests the common sense to wear coats and not lose their God-given joy, despite the cold.

As the mother of the bride kept saying throughout the evening, God is *still* good.

He is our help *and* our shield, agrees the psalmist (Psalm 33:20). Oh, what goodness the Lord grants our hurting world. May we run to Him and be glad at what He offers.

Always, it's all good.

Living Water

Anyone who believes in me
may come and drink!

John 7:38 NLT

The cut flowers came from Ecuador. By the time they arrived at my house, they were droopy and road weary. Instructions said to revive them with a cool drink of refreshing water. Before that, however, the flower stems had to be trimmed so they could drink the water more easily. But would they survive?

The next morning, I discovered my answer. The Ecuadorian bouquet was a glorious sight, featuring blooms I'd never seen before. Fresh water made all the difference—a reminder of what Jesus said about water and what it means to believers.

When Jesus asked a Samaritan woman for a drink of water—implying He'd drink from what she fetched from the well—He changed her life. She was surprised by His request. Jews of that time looked down on Samaritans. But Jesus said, "If you knew the gift of God and who it is that asks you for a drink, you would have asked him and he would have given you living water" (John 4:10). Later, in the temple, He cried out, "Anyone who is thirsty may come to me!" (7:37 NLT). Among those who believed in Him, "'rivers of living water will flow from his heart.' (When he said 'living water,' he was speaking of the Spirit, who would be given to everyone believing in him)" (vv. 38–39 NLT).

God's refreshing Spirit revives us today when we're road weary or life worn. He's the Living Water, dwelling in our souls with holy refreshment. May we drink deep today.

❧❧❧❧❧❧❧❧❧❧❧❧❧

What areas of your life feel parched and dry? What may be preventing you from asking Jesus to give you this living water?

Loving God, when life leaves me road weary and thirsty, thank you for the gift of your Spirit, the Living Water, who dwells in every believer.

John 7:37–39 NLT

On the last day, the climax of the festival, Jesus stood and shouted to the crowds, "Anyone who is thirsty may come to me! Anyone who believes in me may come and drink! For the Scriptures declare, 'Rivers of living water will flow from his heart.'" (When he said "living water," he was speaking of the Spirit, who would be given to everyone believing in him. But the Spirit had not yet been given, because Jesus had not yet entered into his glory.)

From Trash to Treasure

*We have this treasure in jars of clay
to show that this all-surpassing power
is from God and not from us.*

2 Corinthians 4:7

The trash man's house sits atop a steep street in a poor Bogotá neighborhood. Not one thing about it looks special. Yet this unassuming abode in Colombia's capital is home to a free library of twenty-five thousand books—discarded literature that José Alberto Gutiérrez collected to share with poor children in his community.

Local kids crowd into the house during weekend "library hours." Prowling through every room, each packed with books, the children recognize the humble home as more than just Señor José's house—it's a priceless treasury.

The same is true for every follower of Christ. We're made of humble clay—marred by cracks and easily broken. But we're entrusted by God to be a home for His empowering Spirit, who enables us to carry the good news of Christ into a hurting, broken world. It's a big job for ordinary, fragile people.

"We have this treasure in jars of clay to show that this all-surpassing power is from God and not from us" (2 Corinthians 4:7), the apostle Paul told his congregation in the ancient city of Corinth. They were a cross section of people from across this region, so many might have been tempted to "go around preaching about [them]selves," Paul said (v. 5 NLT).

Instead, Paul said, tell others about the priceless One living inside us. It's Him and His all-surpassing power that turns our ordinary lives into a priceless treasury.

▧▧▧▧▧▧▧▧▧▧▧▧

What does it mean to you that you have
a treasure, the Holy Spirit, inside you?
How is it comforting to know that He
enables us to share the good news?

*Jesus, fill up my ordinary life with
the power of your Spirit.*

2 Corinthians 4:5–7

For what we preach is not ourselves, but Jesus Christ as Lord, and ourselves as your servants for Jesus' sake. For God, who said, "Let light shine out of darkness," made his light shine in our hearts to give us the light of the knowledge of God's glory displayed in the face of Christ.

But we have this treasure in jars of clay to show that this all-surpassing power is from God and not from us.

Another Chance

Once again you will have compassion on us.
You will trample our sins under your feet
and throw them into the depths of the ocean!

Micah 7:19 NLT

At the Second Chance Bike Shop near our neighborhood, volunteers rebuild cast-off bicycles and donate them to needy kids. Shop founder Ernie Clark also donates bikes to needy adults, including the homeless, the disabled, and military veterans struggling to make it in civilian life. Not only do the bicycles get a second chance, but sometimes the recipients get a new start too. One veteran used his new bike to pedal to a job interview.

Second chances can transform a person's life, especially when the second chance comes from God. The prophet Micah extolled such grace during a time the nation of Israel gave in to bribery, fraud, and other despicable sins. As Micah lamented, "The godly people have all disappeared; not one honest person is left on the earth" (Micah 7:2 NLT).

God would rightly punish evil, Micah knew. But being loving, He would give those who repented another chance. Humbled by such love, Micah asked, "Where is another God like you, who pardons the guilt of the remnant, overlooking the sins of his special people?" (v. 18 NLT).

We too can rejoice that God doesn't abandon us because of our sins if we ask for forgiveness. As Micah declared of God, "Once again you will have compassion on us. You will trample our sins under your feet and throw them into the depths of the ocean!" (v. 19 NLT).

God's love gives second chances to all who seek Him.

Reflect today on how much God loves you. What sin will you repent of and gain a second chance from our loving God?

Heavenly Father, thank you for giving us the grace of second chances.

Micah 7:1–3, 18–20 NLT

How miserable I am!
I feel like the fruit picker after the
> harvest
> who can find nothing to eat.
Not a cluster of grapes or a single
> early fig
> can be found to satisfy my hunger.
The godly people have all disappeared;
> not one honest person is left on the
> earth.
They are all murderers,
> setting traps even for their own
> brothers.
Both their hands are equally skilled at
> doing evil!
> Officials and judges alike demand
> bribes.
The people with influence get what
> they want,
> and together they scheme to twist
> justice. . . .

Where is another God like you,
    who pardons the guilt of the
        remnant,
    overlooking the sins of his special
        people?
You will not stay angry with your
        people forever,
    because you delight in showing
        unfailing love.
Once again you will have compassion
        on us.
    You will trample our sins under
        your feet
    and throw them into the depths of
        the ocean!
You will show us your faithfulness and
        unfailing love
    as you promised to our ancestors
        Abraham and Jacob long ago.

Strengthened by Song

*I will sing of your strength, in
the morning I will sing of your
love; for you are my fortress.*

Psalm 59:16

When French villagers helped Jewish refugees hide from the Nazis during World War II, some sang songs in the dense forest surrounding their town—letting the refugees know it was safe to come out from hiding. These brave townspeople of Le Chambon-sur-Lignon had answered the call of local pastor André Trocmé and his wife, Magda, to offer wartime refuge to Jews on their windswept plateau known as "La Montagne Protestante." Their musical signal became just one feature of the villagers' bravery that helped save up to three thousand Jews from almost certain death.

In another dangerous time, David sang when his enemy Saul sent nighttime assassins to his house. His use of music wasn't a signal; rather, it was his song of gratitude to God as his refuge. David rejoiced, "I will sing of your strength, in the morning I will sing of your love; for you are my fortress, my refuge in times of trouble" (Psalm 59:16).

Such singing isn't "whistling in the dark" during danger. Instead, David's singing conveyed his trust in almighty God. "You, God, are my fortress, my God on whom I can rely" (v. 17).

David's praise and the villagers' singing in Le Chambon, offer an invitation to bless God today with our singing, making melody to Him despite the worries of life. His loving presence will respond, strengthening our hearts.

How do you feel when you're singing
your favorite praise song? Why do praise
songs inspire us to feel stronger?

Dear God, strengthen my heart with
praises that transform my fears and
worries into worship of you.

Psalm 59:1, 14–17

Deliver me from my enemies, O God;
be my fortress against those who are
attacking me. . . .

They return at evening,
snarling like dogs,
and prowl about the city.
They wander about for food
and howl if not satisfied.
But I will sing of your strength,
in the morning I will sing of your
love;
for you are my fortress,
my refuge in times of trouble.

You are my strength, I sing praise to you;
you, God, are my fortress,
my God on whom I can rely.

The Spirit of Fika

When he was at the table with them,
he took bread, gave thanks, broke
it and began to give it to them.

Luke 24:30

The coffeehouse in the town near my house is named Fika. It's a Swedish word for taking a break with coffee and a pastry, always with family, co-workers, or friends. I'm not Swedish, yet the spirit of fika describes one thing I love most about Jesus—His practice of taking a break to eat and relax with others.

Scholars say Jesus's meals weren't random. Theologian Mark Glanville calls them "the delightful 'second course'" of Israel's feasts and celebrations in the Old Testament. At the table, Jesus lived what God had intended Israel to be: "a center of joy, celebration and justice for the whole world."

From the feeding of five thousand, to the Last Supper—even to the meal with two believers after His resurrection (Luke 24:30)—the table ministry of Jesus invites us to stop our constant striving and abide in Him. Indeed, not until eating with Jesus did the two believers recognize Him as the risen Lord. "He took bread, gave thanks, broke it and began to give it to them. Then their eyes were opened" (vv. 30–31) to the living Christ.

Sitting with a friend recently at Fika, enjoying hot chocolate and rolls, we found ourselves also talking of Jesus. He is the Bread of Life. May we linger at His table and find more of Him.

<hr/>

Make time to eat of the Bread of Life.

Lord, thank you for making time and room for us to abide at your table.

Luke 24:28–35

As they approached the village to which they were going, Jesus continued on as if he were going farther. But they urged him strongly, "Stay with us, for it is nearly evening; the day is almost over." So he went in to stay with them.

When he was at the table with them, he took

bread, gave thanks, broke it and began to give it to them. Then their eyes were opened and they recognized him, and he disappeared from their sight. They asked each other, "Were not our hearts burning within us while he talked with us on the road and opened the Scriptures to us?"

They got up and returned at once to Jerusalem. There they found the Eleven and those with them, assembled together and saying, "It is true! The Lord has risen and has appeared to Simon." Then the two told what had happened on the way, and how Jesus was recognized by them when he broke the bread.

A ROCK IN A WEARY LAND

Her home was in danger. Linda could lose it, get pushed out with no place to go. That giant mountain loomed over a retired Linda after learning her home of twenty years would soon be sold by her landlord—in two short months, in fact—and she'd have to move.

So she'd be on the street. She had nowhere else to live.

"It felt like the world had been pulled from under me," Linda, seventy, told a news reporter. "My house means everything to me."

She'd purchased the property originally but signed it away five years later in a real estate transaction she says she didn't understand. After renting it for another fifteen years, she now faced losing it to a landlord asking $299,000 from her to buy it—more money than Linda could afford.

Her choice? Pay up or get evicted.

"I could not sleep. I could not eat," Linda said. When her landlord told her to vacate the home, she felt like "a stone had just dropped on me. I felt really defeated."*

An impossible situation? Or the kind of hard obstacle where God offers His best help?

We Turn to Him

In Psalm 94, the writer seemed familiar with such obstacles—including heavy-handed opponents and whom to seek when they arise.

> They crush your people, LORD;
> > they oppress your inheritance.
> They slay the widow and the foreigner;
> > they murder the fatherless.
>
> (vv. 5–6)

Linda, who lives alone, certainly understood that kind of attack. So she was led to disclose it to Andrew, a neighbor across the street who works professionally

* Sydney Page, "A Minneapolis Woman Was about to Be Evicted. Neighbors Bought Her Home for Her," *Washington Post*, June 13, 2022, https://www.washingtonpost.com/lifestyle/2022/06/13/eviction-minneapolis-linda-taylor-neighbor/.

as a housing rights organizer. Right away he set out to help Linda keep her home.

"She has always been the one in the neighborhood who greets everyone," he said. She also kept a little free library on her front lawn, filled with books, and volunteered regularly in the community.

Soon, Andrew had collected four hundred signatures from neighbors, all asking the landlord to hold off on eviction and negotiate with Linda so she could buy her home. A fund-raising effort drew donations in amounts of $5 to $15,000, with a local church giving the largest sum—$200,000—making the fund-raising effort a remarkable success.

Again, the psalmist wouldn't be surprised:

> Take notice. . . .
> Does he who fashioned the ear not hear?
>> Does he who formed the eye not see?
> Does he who disciplines nations not
>> punish?
>> Does he who teaches mankind lack
>> knowledge?
>
> (vv. 8–10)

To be sure, "unless the LORD had given me help, I would soon have dwelt in the silence of death," the psalmist added. "When I said, 'My foot is slipping,' your unfailing love, LORD, supported me. When anxiety was great within me, your consolation brought me joy" (vv. 17–19).

Power to Rescue

Such is the rescuing power of the Lord's help in the face of trouble. Sure, "the wicked band together against the righteous and condemn the innocent to death. But the LORD has become my fortress, and my God the rock in whom I take refuge" (vv. 21–22).

May we then be certain that it is proper and right—and spiritually exciting—to seek the Lord's help when we have no place to go and need to be rescued.

But how? Let's simply ask Him: If it be your will, O Lord, rescue me!

He rescues indeed, as only He can. There is no greater rescuer. Therefore, as we wait for His answers, let us celebrate and trust what His Word promises:

> "Because he loves me," says the LORD,
>   "I will rescue him;
> I will protect him, for he acknowl-
>   edges my name.

> He will call on me, and I will answer
> > him;
> > I will be with him in trouble,
> > I will deliver him and honor him.
> > With long life I will satisfy him
> > and show him my salvation."
> > > (Psalm 91:14–16)

The Bible vibrates, indeed, with the stories of people unafraid to ask God for such rescuing help—some of whom are surprising. The pagan king Darius, for example, prayed for God to rescue Daniel, his favorite administrator, from the lion's den because even Darius knew of the power of Daniel's God to save.

"May your God, whom you serve continually, rescue you!" the king declared with passion (Daniel 6:16).

Then, when God did precisely that—rescue Daniel—Darius decreed

> that in every part of my kingdom people must fear and reverence the God of Daniel.
>
> > For he is the living God
> > > and he endures forever;
> > > his kingdom will not be destroyed,
> > > > his dominion will never end.

He rescues and he saves;
> he performs signs and wonders
> in the heavens and on the earth.
He has rescued Daniel
> from the power of the lions.

(vv. 26–27)

Saying this, Darius was saying God's rescue saved both Daniel and him, a pagan king.

Another dramatic Bible rescue?

Rahab the prostitute would have been killed with her family when the Israelites invaded Jericho. But Rahab agreed to hide two Israeli spies who'd snuck into Jericho to size up the enemy—*if* the spies would help spare her family.

Getting rescued would allow Rahab to live with the nation of Israel, whose God she'd hungered to know. "For the LORD your God is God in heaven above and on the earth below" (Joshua 2:11).

On the seventh day of Israel's marching around the city, the Lord gave Jericho into their hands, ordering it destroyed—except for Rahab and her family.

So the young men who had done the spying went in and brought out Rahab, her father and mother, her brothers and sisters and all who belonged to her.

They brought out her entire family and put them in a place outside the camp of Israel. (6:23)

More dramatic, of course, is that Rahab is listed by name in the New Testament among the great names of faith (Hebrews 11:31)—and also among the lineage of Jesus, as the mother of Boaz. And who is he? "Boaz [was] the father of Obed, whose mother was Ruth, Obed the father of Jesse, and Jesse the father of King David" (Matthew 1:5–6).

God's rescue of us is life-changing, miraculous intervention.

It's an exciting reminder that when God rescues us, He follows it with redemption, transformation, and salvation that can bless for generations.

In this way, rescue isn't just a nice favor done for us by God. God's rescue of us is life-changing, miraculous intervention.

Linda, the homeowner, confirms this, saying she was "stunned" by the support of neighbors, friends, family, and the generous church who helped save her house.

"When that came through, my faith grew bigger than a mountain," Linda was quoted in a news article.

Rescuing isn't idle help. So when we need rescuing, may we have the courage to ask God to send it, allowing us to stand firm on the Rock. Whatever happens, our lives will transform and grow. But even more, so will the salvaged strength of our once feeble faith.

Trusting God's Foresight

[The magi] returned to their
country by another route.

Matthew 2:12

While driving us to an unfamiliar location, my husband noticed that the GPS directions suddenly seemed wrong. After entering a reliable four-lane highway, we were advised to exit and travel along a one-lane frontage road running parallel to us. "I'll just trust it," Dan said, despite seeing no delays. After about ten miles, however, the traffic on the highway next to us slowed to a near standstill. The trouble? Major construction. And the frontage road? With little traffic, it provided a clear path to our destination. "I couldn't see ahead," Dan said, "but the GPS could"—as we agreed, "just like God can."

Knowing what was ahead, God in a dream gave a similar change in directions to the wise men who'd come from the east to worship Jesus, "king of the Jews" (Matthew 2:2). King Herod, disturbed by the news of a "rival" king, lied to the magi, sending them to Bethlehem, saying: "Go to Bethlehem and search carefully for the child. And when you find him, come back and tell me so that I can go and worship him, too!" (v. 8 NLT). Warned in a dream not to go back to Herod, however, "they returned to their country by another route" (v. 12).

God will guide our steps too. As we travel life's highways, we can trust that He sees ahead and remain confident that "he will make [our] paths straight" as we submit to His directions (Proverbs 3:6).

Recall a time when God presented you with a change in your life's direction. As you trusted Him, what was the outcome?

I can't see the road ahead, God, as you can. Please give me discernment to know when a change in direction is coming from you.

Matthew 2:1–2, 7–12 NLT

Jesus was born in Bethlehem in Judea, during the reign of King Herod. About that time some wise men from eastern lands arrived in Jerusalem, asking,

"Where is the newborn king of the Jews? We saw his star as it rose, and we have come to worship him." . . .

Then Herod called for a private meeting with the wise men, and he learned from them the time when the star first appeared. Then he told them, "Go to Bethlehem and search carefully for the child. And when you find him, come back and tell me so that I can go and worship him, too!"

After this interview the wise men went their way. And the star they had seen in the east guided them to Bethlehem. It went ahead of them and stopped over the place where the child was. When they saw the star, they were filled with joy! They entered the house and saw the child with his mother, Mary, and they bowed down and worshiped him. Then they opened their treasure chests and gave him gifts of gold, frankincense, and myrrh.

When it was time to leave, they returned to their own country by another route, for God had warned them in a dream not to return to Herod.

Hearing Christ, Not Chaos

My sheep listen to my voice.
John 10:27

After watching cable news for hours each day, the elderly man grew agitated and anxious—worried the world was falling apart and taking him with it. "Please turn it off," his grown daughter begged him. "Just stop listening." But the man continued to spend disturbing amounts of time on social media and other news sources.

What we listen to matters deeply. We see this in Jesus's encounter with Pontius Pilate. Responding to criminal charges brought against Jesus by religious leaders, Pilate summoned Him and asked, "Are you the king of the Jews" (John 18:33). Jesus replied with a stunning question: "Is that your own idea . . . or did others talk to you about me?" (v. 34).

The same question tests us. In a world of panic, are we listening to chaos or to Christ? Indeed, "my sheep listen to my voice," He said. "I know them, and they follow me" (10:27). Jesus used this illustration to explain Himself to doubting religious leaders. As with a good shepherd, He said that "his sheep follow him because they know his voice. But they will never follow a stranger; in fact, they will run away from him because they do not recognize a stranger's voice" (vv. 4–5).

As our Good Shepherd, Jesus bids us to hear Him above all. May we listen well and find His peace.

XXXXXXXXXXXXXX

What do you hear on the news or social media that makes you feel anxious? How can you give more time to hearing the voice of God?

Loving God, in a noisy world, when you speak to my heart, mind, and spirit in and through the Scriptures, may I hear you over all.

John 10:1–7, 27 NLT

"I tell you the truth, anyone who sneaks over the wall of a sheepfold, rather than going through the gate, must surely be a thief and a robber! But the one who enters through the gate is the shepherd of the sheep. The gatekeeper opens the gate for him, and the sheep recognize his voice and come to him. He calls his own sheep by name and leads them out. After he has gathered his own flock, he walks ahead of them, and they follow him because they know his voice. They won't follow a stranger; they will run from him because they don't know his voice."

Those who heard Jesus use this illustration didn't understand what he meant, so he explained it to them: "I tell you the truth, I am the gate for the sheep. . . .

"My sheep listen to my voice; I know them, and they follow me."

Enjoying Beauty

God has made everything
beautiful for its own time.

Ecclesiastes 3:11 NLT

The painting caught my eye like almost none before. Displayed along a long hallway in a big city hospital, its deep pastel hues and Navajo Native American figures were so arresting I stopped to marvel and stare. "Look at *that*," I whispered to my husband, Dan.

He was walking ahead, but I hesitated, bypassing other paintings on the wall to gaze only at this one. "Beautiful," I concluded.

Many things in life are beautiful indeed. Master paintings. Scenic vistas. Inspired crafts. But so is a child's smile. A friend's hello. A robin's blue egg. A seashell's strong ridges. To relieve the burdens life can bring, "[God] has made everything beautiful in its time" (Ecclesiastes 3:11). In such beauty, Bible scholars explain, we get a glimpse of the perfection of God's creation—including the glory of His perfect rule to come.

We can only imagine such perfection, so God grants

us a foretaste through life's beauty. In this way, God "has planted eternity in the human heart" (v. 11 NLT). Some days life looks drab and futile. But God mercifully provides moments of beauty to spark awe and wonder.

The artist of the painting I admired, Gerard Curtis Delano, understood that. "God [gave] me a talent to create beauty," he once said, "and this is what He wanted me to do."

Seeing such beauty, how can we respond? We can thank God for eternity to come while pausing to enjoy the glory we already see.

〰〰〰〰〰〰〰〰〰

How do you respond to the beauty
God has placed in this world? How
does beauty reflect Him?

*Father, help me in the moments of the day
to see and enjoy the beauty you bring into
my life as I also look forward to eternity.*

Ecclesiastes 3:9–13 NLT

What do people really get for all their hard work?
I have seen the burden God has placed on us all.

Yet God has made everything beautiful for its own time. He has planted eternity in the human heart, but even so, people cannot see the whole scope of God's work from beginning to end. So I concluded there is nothing better than to be happy and enjoy ourselves as long as we can. And people should eat and drink and enjoy the fruits of their labor, for these are gifts from God.

Just as I Am

*Jesus called his twelve disciples to
him and gave them authority.*

Matthew 10:1

The young woman couldn't sleep. A person with a lifelong physical disability, she'd be center stage at a church bazaar the next day to receive donations to pay for her higher education. But I'm not worthy, Charlotte Elliott reasoned. Tossing and turning, she doubted her credentials, questioning every aspect of her spiritual life. Still restless the next day, she finally moved to a desk to pick up pen and paper and write down the words of the now classic hymn, "Just as I Am":

> Just as I am, without one plea
> But that thy blood was shed for me
> And that thou bidst me come to thee
> O Lamb of God, I come, I come.

Her words, written in 1835, express how Jesus called His disciples to come and serve Him. Not because they were ready. They weren't. But because He authorized them—just as they were. A ragtag group, his team of twelve included a tax collector, a zealot, two overly ambitious brothers (see Mark 10:35–37), and Judas Iscariot, who later betrayed him. Still, He gave them authority to "heal the sick, raise the dead, cure those with leprosy, and cast out demons" (Matthew 10:8 NLT)—all without taking any money, luggage, extra shirt or sandals, or even a walking stick with them (vv. 9–10).

"I am sending you," He said (v. 16), and He was enough. For each of us who say yes to Him, He still is.

~~~~~~~~~~~~~~~~~~~~~

What's your current situation or status in life? What doubts have you expressed about your readiness to be used by God?

Jesus, bid me to come to you,
fully dependent on your grace and
power to make a difference.

Matthew 10:1, 5–10, 16–20 NLT

Jesus called his twelve disciples together and gave them authority to cast out evil spirits and to heal every kind of disease and illness. . . .

Jesus sent [them out] with these instructions: "Don't go to the Gentiles or the Samaritans, but only to the people of Israel—God's lost sheep. Go and announce to them that the Kingdom of Heaven is near. Heal the sick, raise the dead, cure those with leprosy, and cast out demons. Give as freely as you have received!

"Don't take any money in your money belts—no gold, silver, or even copper coins. Don't carry a traveler's bag with a change of clothes and sandals or even a walking stick. Don't hesitate to accept hospitality, because those who work deserve to be fed. . . .

"Look, I am sending you out as sheep among wolves. So be as shrewd as snakes and harmless as doves. But beware! For you will be handed over to the courts and will be flogged with whips in the synagogues. You will stand trial before governors and kings because you are my followers. But this will be your opportunity to tell the rulers and other unbelievers about me. When you are arrested, don't worry about how to respond or what to say. God will give you the right words at the right time. For it is not you who will be speaking—it will be the Spirit of your Father speaking through you."

He Knows Your Name

I have summoned you by
name; you are mine.

Isaiah 43:1

After having broken with our longtime church, my husband and I reunited with the fellowship after three long years. But how would people treat us? Would they welcome us back? Love us? Forgive us for leaving? We got our answer on a sunny Sunday morning. As we walked through the big church doors, we kept hearing our names. "Pat! Dan! It's so great to see you!" As children's author Kate DiCamillo wrote in one of her popular books, "Reader, nothing is sweeter in this sad world than the sound of someone you love calling your name."

The same assurance was true for the people of Israel. We had chosen a different church for a time, but the Israelites had turned their backs on God. Yet He welcomed them back. He sent the prophet Isaiah to assure them, "Do not fear, for I have redeemed you; I have summoned you by name; you are mine" (Isaiah 43:1).

In this world where we can feel unseen, unappreciated, and even unknown, be assured that God knows each of us by name. "You are precious and honored in my sight," He promises (v. 4). "When you pass through the waters, I will be with you; and when you pass through the rivers, they will not sweep over you" (v. 2). This promise isn't just for Israel. Jesus gave His life to ransom us. He knows our names. Why? In love, we are His.

<hr />

Why does God welcome His people
back to Him? How has He shown
that He knows you by name?

Jesus, when I stray from your arms and
your fellowship, summon me home by
name. I'm so grateful to be yours.

Isaiah 43:1–7

> But now, this is what the LORD says—
>   he who created you, Jacob,
>   he who formed you, Israel:

"Do not fear, for I have redeemed you;
    I have summoned you by name; you
        are mine.
When you pass through the waters,
    I will be with you;
and when you pass through the rivers,
    they will not sweep over you.
When you walk through the fire,
    you will not be burned;
    the flames will not set you ablaze.
For I am the LORD your God,
    the Holy One of Israel, your Savior;
I give Egypt for your ransom,
    Cush and Seba in your stead.
Since you are precious and honored in
        my sight,
    and because I love you,
I will give people in exchange for you,
    nations in exchange for your life.
Do not be afraid, for I am with you;
    I will bring your children from the
        east
    and gather you from the west.
I will say to the north, 'Give them up!'

and to the south, 'Do not hold them
    back.'
Bring my sons from afar
    and my daughters from the ends of
        the earth—
everyone who is called by my name,
    whom I created for my glory,
    whom I formed and made."

A RIVER IN DRY PLACES

I'm sitting at my desk watching the clock and calendar. Two ministry deadlines are breathing down my neck. That's how it feels anyway. So I've run out of rope and hope. Not enough time. Too little mental space. How can I possibly finish both assignments and do them well? Worried, fidgety, and overwhelmed, I ask friends to pray for me. Praying for myself too, I ask the Lord to inspire me to find enough time and insight to meet my obligations.

Then, suddenly, the first deadline is put on hold. A four-week window blows wide open in my schedule, as if released by a fresh wind.

It feels like a gift.

Reflecting with my husband on what happened, I share my simple conclusion. "The Lord provided the time I needed. Simply. He helped."

Paul described this kind of provision when he was

in need—not of time but of money. Monetary gifts, in fact, are often the focus when the subject is godly provision. In this season, I needed time to finish ministry work, but Paul acknowledged spiritual workers also have material needs, money among them. As Paul said, he knew how to be content regardless of his basic needs, "whether it is with a full stomach or empty, with plenty or little. For I can do everything through Christ, who gives me strength" (Philippians 4:12–13 NLT).

"Even so," he told the generous church members at Philippi, "you have done well to share with me in my present difficulty" (v. 14 NLT). He didn't say that to prompt more gifts. "At the moment I have all I need—and more! I am generously supplied with the gifts you sent me. . . . They are a sweet-smelling sacrifice that is acceptable and pleasing to God" (v. 18 NLT).

Then Paul made a stunning declaration.

The Provision of Help

"This same God who takes care of me will supply all your needs from his glorious riches, which have been given to us in Christ Jesus" (v. 19 NLT).

It's a remarkable proclamation—that this same

God who so carefully cared for Paul through the provisions of God's people will take care of us, supplying all our basic, humble needs in the same helping, loving way.

Reading Paul's letter on my time-crunched afternoon, I was struck by two things. First, Paul is convinced. He is certain. The Lord *will* provide for His people's needs, the bold apostle writes. Second, Paul declares the Lord's provisions *will* spring from His glorious riches, "which have been given to us in Christ Jesus" (v. 19).

This same God who so carefully cared for Paul through the provisions of God's people will take care of us.

There's no limit, that is, to the provisions available to us. Those riches in Christ include our simple needs, such as the gift of time—which, at first, didn't seem to me glorious enough. The extra time I needed seemed, at its heart, too ordinary and practical.

But as I considered, the everyday practicality of ordinary provision became for me the most important gift to celebrate.

"Give us today our daily bread," Jesus taught in

Matthew 6:11. The request shows our dependence on our God—who, in this way, tells us not to worry about our daily need to eat good food.

As for time, "Teach us to number our days, that we may gain a heart of wisdom" (Psalm 90:12). This is Moses's prayer, noting that time isn't just a practical matter. Time is priceless.

"Our days may come to seventy years," Moses prayed, "or eighty, if our strength endures" (v. 10) . . . but relent, he asks God, and give us more time and more favor (vv. 13, 17).

> Satisfy us in the morning with your
> unfailing love,
> that we may sing for joy and be
> glad all our days.
> Make us glad for as many days as you
> have afflicted us,
> for as many years as we have seen
> trouble.
> May your deeds be shown to your
> servants,
> your splendor to their children.
>
> May the favor of the Lord our God rest
> on us;

establish the work of our hands for
 us—
yes, establish the work of our
 hands.

(vv. 14–17)

What beautiful, bright requests by Moses for provision.

Provision for what? Joy, gladness, knowledge of God by our children and others. Wisdom and physical strength too. Indeed, *may your favor rest on us, Lord*. Then, *establish the work of our hands* to give us success and a legacy (Genesis 24:42; Nehemiah 1:11; Psalm 118:25).

Yet More Provision

Other servants of God asked for and received those same glorious spiritual gifts and others as well—peace (John 14:27); hope, compassion, and faithfulness (Lamentations 3:21–23); comfort (2 Corinthians 1:4); power, love, and self-discipline (2 Timothy 1:7).

Not a single thing, in fact, is beyond the provision of God. He "has blessed us in the heavenly realms with every spiritual blessing in Christ" (Ephesians 1:3).

It's so easy to forget the simple power of this

provisional truth. To help myself remember, I open my prayer journal and write a note on the gratitude list I keep daily to remind myself of the basic beauty God is providing:

Rain today. In my parched area, we really need it.

A spirit of joy and connection at a book club talk I agreed to give.

Renewal of a lost friendship.

Wisdom to plan ahead—and to pack up my car and gas it up for a short road trip scheduled for the next days.

Then I laugh. My next reminder could seem silly, but I thank God also for . . .

Showing me my car keys when I suddenly couldn't find them.

Such small things? But shouldn't God's provision mean only "big" things—such as financial help? The kind of help Paul was writing about in his letter?

God does indeed provide us with financial assistance, including the ability "to produce wealth" (Deuteronomy 8:18). This gift, however, isn't for our own gratification. Our blessings are meant to bless others. For even "the Son of Man did not come to be served, but to serve, and to give his life as a ransom for many" (Matthew 20:28).

I share that verse for perspective—to help me first see God's provision in small matters, such as His help to find my car keys. But later, looking on my phone at photos from a library event where I spoke, I noticed another beautiful thing: God provided His joy.

I look so happy in the photos—joyous to be serving and sharing, even with people whom, one day before, I didn't even know.

God knew I needed that joy, and God graciously provided it. As Paul wrote, His unlimited character means He is "able to do immeasurably more than all we ask or imagine, according to his power that is at work within us" (Ephesians 3:20).

Car keys. Joy. Rain. Money to pay a bill—plus more to bless someone else. What a help to receive such loving provision. May we look for it every day, starting from the moment we open our grateful eyes.

A World of Provision

There is the sea, vast and spacious,
teeming with creatures beyond number.

Psalm 104:25

It's 2:00 a.m. when Nadia, a farmer of sea cucumbers, walks into a roped-off pen in the ocean shallows near her Madagascar village to harvest her "crop." The early hour doesn't bother her. "Life was very hard before I started farming," she says. "I didn't have any source of income." Now, as a member of a marine-protection program called Velondriake, meaning "to live with the sea," Nadia sees her income growing and stabilizing. "We thank God that this project appeared," she adds.

It emerged in large part because God's creation provided what her project needs—a natural supply of sea life to harvest. In praise of our providing God, the psalmist wrote, "He makes grass grow for the cattle, and plants for people to cultivate" (Psalm 104:14). As well, "there is the sea . . . teeming with creatures beyond number—living things both large and small" (v. 25).

It's a wonder, indeed, how God's wondrous creation also provides for us. The humble sea cucumber, for example, helps form a healthy marine food chain. And careful harvesting of sea cucumbers grants Nadia and her neighbors a living wage.

Nothing is random in God's creation. He uses it all for His glory and our good. Thus, "I will sing to the LORD all my life," says the psalmist (v. 33). We too can praise Him today as we ponder all that He provides.

〰〰〰〰〰〰〰〰〰〰

In what ways does God provide for you through His creation? How can you thank Him for that today?

O Creator God, we're humbled by your vast creation and all the ways you provide for our needs.

Psalm 104:10–18, 24–26

He makes springs pour water into the ravines;
it flows between the mountains.

They give water to all the beasts of the
        field;
    the wild donkeys quench their thirst.
The birds of the sky nest by the waters;
    they sing among the branches.
He waters the mountains from his
        upper chambers;
    the land is satisfied by the fruit of
        his work.
He makes grass grow for the cattle,
    and plants for people to cultivate—
    bringing forth food from the earth:
wine that gladdens human hearts,
    oil to make their faces shine,
    and bread that sustains their hearts.
The trees of the LORD are well watered,
    the cedars of Lebanon that he
        planted.
There the birds make their nests;
    the stork has its home in the
        junipers.
The high mountains belong to the wild
        goats;
    the crags are a refuge for the
        hyrax. . . .

How many are your works, LORD!
In wisdom you have made them all;
the earth is full of your creatures.
There is the sea, vast and spacious,
teeming with creatures beyond
number—
living things both large and small.
There the ships go to and fro,
and Leviathan, which you formed
to frolic there.

Rich toward God

Godliness with contentment is great gain.
1 Timothy 6:6

Growing up during the Great Depression, my parents knew deep hardship as children. As a result, they were thrifty adults—hardworking and grateful money stewards. At the same time, they were never greedy. They gave time, talent, and treasure to their church, charity groups, and the needy. Indeed, they handled their money wisely and gave cheerfully.

As believers in Jesus, my parents took to heart the apostle Paul's warning: "Those who want to get rich fall into temptation and a trap and into many foolish and harmful desires that plunge people into ruin and destruction" (1 Timothy 6:9).

Paul gave this advice to Timothy, the young pastor in Ephesus, a wealthy city where riches tempted rich and poor alike.

"The love of money is a root of all kinds of evil," Paul warned. "Some people, eager for money, have wandered from the faith and pierced themselves with many griefs" (v. 10).

What, then, is the antidote to greed? Being rich toward God, said Jesus (Luke 12:13–21). By pursuing, appreciating, and loving our heavenly Father above all, He remains our chief delight. As the psalmist wrote, "Satisfy us in the morning with your unfailing love, that we may sing for joy and be glad all our days" (Psalm 90:14).

Rejoicing in Him daily relieves us of coveting, leaving us contented. May Jesus redeem our heart's desires, making us rich toward God!

How have you mishandled money
or made it more than it ought to be?
How might you give your financial
concerns to God this day?

*Satisfy us in the morning, God, with
your unfailing love—replacing our
greed with holy hunger for you.*

1 Timothy 6:6–11

But godliness with contentment is great gain. For we brought nothing into the world, and we can take nothing out of it. But if we have food and clothing, we will be content with that. Those who want to get rich fall into temptation and a trap and into many foolish and harmful desires that plunge people into ruin and destruction. For the love of money is a root of all kinds of evil. Some people, eager for money, have wandered from the faith and pierced themselves with many griefs.

But you, man of God, flee from all this, and pursue righteousness, godliness, faith, love, endurance and gentleness.

From Pity to Praise

*The Lord stood at my side
and gave me strength.*

2 Timothy 4:17

At a coat drive for children, excited kids searched gratefully for their favorite colors and proper sizes. They also gained self-esteem, an organizer said, with new coats boosting their acceptance by peers and school attendance on winter days.

The apostle Paul seemed to need a coat as well when he wrote to Timothy, "Bring the cloak that I left with Carpus at Troas" (2 Timothy 4:13). Held in a cold Roman prison, Paul needed warmth but also companionship. "No one came to my support, but everyone deserted me," he lamented, when he faced a Roman judge (v. 16). His words pierce our hearts with the honesty of this great missionary's pain.

Yet in these final words of Paul's last recorded letter—his closing thoughts after an astounding ministry—he moves from pity to praise. "But the Lord stood at my side," he adds (v. 17), and his words rally our hearts. As Paul declared, "[God] gave me strength so that I might preach the Good News in its entirety for all the Gentiles to hear. And he rescued me from certain death" (v. 17 NLT).

If you're facing a crisis, lacking even the right clothing for warmth or close friends to help, remember God. He's faithful to revive, provide, and deliver. Why? For His glory and for our purpose in His kingdom.

※※※※※※※※※※※※

In what "cold" area of your life do you need God's great and warming strength? As you praise Him, how does your outlook change?

Our strong God, when life's circumstances overwhelm us, stand with us and stir our praise, giving us your strength to overcome.

2 Timothy 4:9–18

Do your best to come to me quickly, for Demas, because he loved this world, has deserted me and has gone to Thessalonica. Crescens has gone to Galatia, and Titus to Dalmatia. Only Luke is with me. Get Mark and bring him with you, because he is helpful to me in my ministry. I sent Tychicus to Ephesus. When you come, bring the cloak that I left with Carpus at Troas, and my scrolls, especially the parchments.

Alexander the metalworker did me a great deal of harm. The Lord will repay him for what he has done. You too should be on your guard against him, because he strongly opposed our message.

At my first defense, no one came to my support, but everyone deserted me. May it not be held against them. But the Lord stood at my side and gave me strength, so that through me the message might be fully proclaimed and all the Gentiles might hear it. And I was delivered from the lion's mouth. The Lord will rescue me from every evil attack and will bring me safely to his heavenly kingdom. To him be glory for ever and ever. Amen.

Laundry Day

Go, then, to all peoples everywhere
and make them my disciples.

Matthew 28:19 GNT

Driving through a low-income area near his church, Colorado pastor Chad Graham started praying for his "neighbors." When he noticed a small laundromat, he stopped to look inside and found it filled with customers. One asked Graham for a spare coin to operate the clothes dryer. That small request inspired a weekly "Laundry Day" sponsored by Graham's church. Members donate coins and soap to the laundromat, pray with customers, and support the owner of the laundry facility.

Their neighborhood outreach, which dares to include a laundromat, reflects Jesus's Great Commission to His disciples. As He said, "I have been given all authority in heaven and on earth. Go, then, to all peoples everywhere and make them my disciples: baptize them in the name of the Father, the Son, and the Holy Spirit" (Matthew 28:18–19 GNT).

His Holy Spirit's powerful presence enables "everywhere" outreach, including even a laundromat. Indeed, we don't go alone. As Jesus promised, "I will be with you always, to the end of the age" (v. 20 GNT).

Pastor Chad experienced that truth after praying at the laundromat for a customer named Jeff who was battling cancer. As Chad reported, "When we opened our eyes, every customer in the room was praying with us, hands stretched out toward Jeff. It was one of the most sacred moments I have experienced as a pastor."

The lesson? Let's go everywhere to proclaim Christ.

<hr/>

Where can you go in your neighborhood
today to proclaim Christ? How could
His powerful presence enable you?

*Jesus, enable me to proclaim your
good news today—everywhere.*

Matthew 28:16–20

Then the eleven disciples went to Galilee, to the mountain where Jesus had told them to go. When they saw him, they worshiped him; but some doubted. Then Jesus came to them and said, "All authority in heaven and on earth has been given to me. Therefore go and make disciples of all nations, baptizing them in the name of the Father and of the Son and of the Holy Spirit, and teaching them to obey everything I have commanded you. And surely I am with you always, to the very end of the age."

A Humble Snack

Clothe yourselves with humility.
1 Peter 5:5

The bag of snack chips was small, but it taught an American missionary a big lesson. Working one evening in the Dominican Republic, she had arrived at a church meeting and opened her chips when a woman she hardly knew reached and grabbed a few from the bag. Others helped themselves too.

How rude, the missionary thought. Then she realized a humbling lesson. She didn't yet understand the culture where she'd agreed to serve. Rather than emphasizing individualism, as in the United States, she learned that life in the Dominican Republic is lived in community. Sharing one's food and goods is how people relate to each other. Her way wasn't better, just different. She confessed, "It was very humbling to discover these things about me." As she began to recognize her own cultural biases, she also learned that humbly sharing with others helped her serve them better.

Peter taught this lesson to church leaders: treat others with humility. He counseled the elders to resist "lording it over those entrusted to you" (1 Peter 5:3). And those younger? "Submit yourselves to your elders. All of you, clothe yourselves with humility"—for, as he declared, "God opposes the proud but shows favor to the humble" (v. 5). Therefore, "humble yourselves . . . under God's mighty hand, that he may lift you up in due time" (v. 6).

May He help us humbly live before Him and others today.

What cultural biases do you harbor?
How could you let God transform those
attitudes so you humbly serve all?

*Father, exchange my arrogance regarding
others with your humble love.*

1 Peter 5:1–6

To the elders among you, I appeal as a fellow elder and a witness of Christ's sufferings who also will share in the glory to be revealed: Be shepherds of

God's flock that is under your care, watching over them—not because you must, but because you are willing, as God wants you to be; not pursuing dishonest gain, but eager to serve; not lording it over those entrusted to you, but being examples to the flock. And when the Chief Shepherd appears, you will receive the crown of glory that will never fade away.

In the same way, you who are younger, submit yourselves to your elders. All of you, clothe yourselves with humility toward one another, because,

> "God opposes the proud
>> but shows favor to the humble."

Humble yourselves, therefore, under God's mighty hand, that he may lift you up in due time.

A BRIDGE OVER TROUBLED WATER

This isn't good. Not right either. I'm on my phone arguing with a family member. It's a real standoff. He and I are both in our corners, taking hard stands on a family problem where we disagree. So we won't budge, neither of us. For two low-conflict people—close relatives who rarely argue with anybody, let alone each other—we must sound a bit out of our minds.

My husband walks into the room, in fact. He gives me a look: What's going on?

I respond with a deep frown, showing him my frustration. The call ends after too long—and without resolution.

Later the bickering picks up again by text. Messages fly back and forth for almost an hour. Do other people do this? This slugfest by phone? A digital fistfight? What a nightmare. Finally we both back off a bit.

I say something to calm the waters. He does too. But we're still miles apart in how we see this problem.

Later that night, when my mind is still racing— still upset by the argument and our inability to solve it—I tiptoe into my little home office and open my prayer journal.

Prayer is certainly the best place for me to start. As my pastor says, tension is holy. "Because it's borne," he says, "out of love and relationship."

All of that seems on the line. So I write these words in my prayer journal: "Lord, help!" My family tiff needs a divine breakthrough, for sure—so I ask the Lord for His guidance, writing down the request with weariness but, just as resolutely, with faith.

God already knows the answer I can't yet fathom.

God knows best, I am certain, in this family matter— even if I don't yet see a way out. But God does. God already knows the answer I can't yet fathom. I consider the reasons why.

First, God is omniscient. He knows all things—"the end from the beginning, from ancient times, what is

182

still to come. I say, 'My purpose will stand, and I will do all that I please'" (Isaiah 46:10).

Thus, He knows and can see my family circumstance from every angle. What looks to me like a hopeless standoff is, to Him, already solved.

His knowing is a stunning expression of His love. Then, even "if our hearts condemn us, we know that God is greater than our hearts, and he knows everything" (1 John 3:20).

Thus, *His* solution is what I seek. So I pray: Show me your way in this, heavenly Father. Help me see what you already know.

Here's what I do know: "In all things God works for the good of those who love him, who have been called according to his purpose" (Romans 8:28). And it doesn't take long for God's knowing in this situation to emerge. In a sort of step-by-step fashion, I find myself waking up the next morning to what feels like a door opening on a solution. So I sit with it for a moment, remembering the second reason God knows best:

God *is* love. So He wants His best for us—all of us. That includes my family and, specifically, the two of us who are at odds over a snarl of an issue—unless we can think out of the box, closer to what God already knows is best.

I call my family member, who listens to my humble suggestion. To both of us it seems wildly brave and unusual—maybe even off-the-wall. But neither of us turns away from it. Turning instead to God in love, we seem to find more love in each other.

Even better, when I share the solution with a third family member, her response is like icing on the cake. It completes the idea I've proposed, but in a stronger, bolder way—one which could bless all in our small family plus bring us closer in a fresh way. And so I'm reminded of a third reason why God knows best:

He wants us to experience His abundant life. Not barely-squeaking-by life. Not a life of settling and saying, Well, okay, that'll have to do.

Instead, Jesus said that while "the thief comes only to steal and kill and destroy . . . I came that [you] may have life and have it abundantly" (John 10:10 ESV).

That verse used to worry me. It sounded like prosperity gospel—a theology I ran from as fast as my sanctified feet could carry me. Then I learned the truth about abundance.

When Jesus spoke of it, He was inviting us to an abundance of spiritual gifts—His peace, hope, love, forgiveness, joy, and guidance among other gifts, as well as eternal life.

Do we trust Him to help us discover those things? Indeed, the best for us?

For me, that's what it came down to in the situation I've been describing: trusting God—especially when my human-made plan seemed to unravel.

I'd been so excited and hopeful, after thrashing through a family problem, that three or four of us had figured out the best solution. Not quite. But poised over my prayer journal, I wrote that I could see something happening. First, the Lord had a different timetable. Second, we needed to "be still" and know that He is God, working out His best for us in a potentially inflammatory family situation.

Oh, I wanted Him to move fast. Fast and clear. But things had slowed to a crawl, and we all needed to slow down with God and move at His blessed pace.

Did we trust Him for *slow* help? Did I? I've been shouting to the skies throughout this devotional book that I do trust the Lord, no matter His pace. Now, however, it was time to stop writing that message and live it. But even if I couldn't see it yet?

That's when His help matters most, I have learned. It says there's something so good and remarkable that we can't see, think, or imagine what it might be. Not yet.

In the meantime, may we all know this for certain. God's help—from God our Helper—may not be what we expected. It will be better.

But for now, let us rejoice! God's best help is surely on its way.

Game of Change

Love your enemies.
Luke 6:27

The handshake spoke volumes. On a March night in 1963, two college basketball players—one Black, one White—defied the hate of segregationists and shook hands, marking the first time in Mississippi State's history that its all-White men's team played against an integrated team. To compete in the "game of change" against Loyola University Chicago in a national tournament, the Mississippi State squad avoided an injunction to stop them by using decoy players to leave their state. Loyola's Black players, meantime, had endured racial slurs all season, getting pelted with popcorn and ice, and faced closed doors while traveling.

Yet the young men played. The Loyola Ramblers beat the Mississippi State Bulldogs 61–51, and Loyola eventually went on to win the NCAA national championship. But what really won that night? A move from hate toward love. As Jesus taught, "Love your enemies, do good to those who hate you" (Luke 6:27).

God's instruction was a life-changing concept. To love our enemies as Christ taught, we must obey His revolutionary mandate to change. As Paul wrote, "If anyone is in Christ, the new creation has come: The old has gone, the new is here!" (2 Corinthians 5:17). But how does His new way in us defeat the old? With love. Then, in each other, we can finally see Him.

⁓⁓⁓⁓⁓⁓⁓⁓⁓⁓⁓⁓⁓

In your life, what leads you to see others as enemies? What changes can you make to confront hate with Jesus's love?

Help me, loving God, to see others not as enemies but as your precious people to love like Jesus does.

Luke 6:27–31

But to you who are listening I say: Love your enemies, do good to those who hate you, bless those who curse you, pray for those who mistreat you. If someone slaps you on one cheek, turn to them the other also. If someone takes your coat, do not withhold your shirt from them. Give to everyone who asks you, and if anyone takes what belongs to you, do not demand it back. Do to others as you would have them do to you.

Recovering What's Lost

David found strength in the LORD his God.
1 Samuel 30:6 NLT

At the cell phone store, the young pastor steeled himself for bad news. His smartphone, accidentally dropped during our Bible class, was a total loss, right? Actually, no. The store clerk recovered all the pastor's data, including his Bible videos and photos. She also recovered "every photo I'd ever deleted," the pastor said. The store also "replaced my broken phone with a brand-new phone." As he said, "I recovered all I had lost and more."

David once led his own recovery mission after an attack by the vicious Amalekites. Spurned by Philistine rulers, David and his army discovered the Amalekites had raided and burned down their town of Ziklag. "They had carried off the women and children and everyone else. . . . When David and his men saw the ruins and realized what had happened to their families, they wept until they could weep no more" (1 Samuel 30:2–4 NLT).

The soldiers were so bitter with their leader that they talked of stoning him. "But David found strength in the LORD his God" (v. 6 NLT). After seeking God's counsel, David pursued the Amalekites, and as God promised, "David got back everything the Amalekites had taken, and he rescued his two wives. Nothing was missing: small or great, son or daughter, nor anything else that had been taken. David brought everything back" (vv. 18–19 NLT).

As we face spiritual attacks that rob us even of hope, may we find renewed strength in God. He will be with us in every challenge of life.

What spiritual attacks or life loss are you experiencing? Turning from your despair to God, how will you find renewed strength in Him?

God, help me to find hope in you even as I face life's challenges.

1 Samuel 30:1–6, 18–19 NLT

Three days later, when David and his men arrived home at their town of Ziklag, they found that the Amalekites had made a raid into the Negev and Ziklag; they had crushed Ziklag and burned it to the ground. They had carried off the women and children and everyone else but without killing anyone.

When David and his men saw the ruins and realized what had happened to their families, they wept until they could weep no more. David's two wives, Ahinoam from Jezreel and Abigail, the widow of Nabal from Carmel, were among those captured. David was now in great danger because all his men were very bitter about losing their sons and daughters, and they began to talk of stoning him. But David found strength in the Lord his God. . . .

David got back everything the Amalekites had taken, and he rescued his two wives. Nothing was missing: small or great, son or daughter, nor anything else that had been taken. David brought everything back.

First Forgive

Esau ran to meet Jacob and embraced him.
Genesis 33:4

We called ourselves sisters in Christ, but my White friend and I had begun to act like enemies. Over a café breakfast one morning, we argued unkindly over our differing racial and political views. Then we parted, with me vowing not to see her again. One year later, however, we were hired by the same ministry—working in the same department, unable not to reconnect. Awkwardly at first, we talked over conflicts. Then over time, God helped us apologize to each other, heal, and give the ministry our best.

God also healed the bitter division between Esau and his twin brother, Jacob, and blessed both their lives. A onetime schemer, Jacob had robbed Esau of their father's blessing. But twenty years later, God called Jacob to return to their homeland. So Jacob sent ahead bountiful gifts to appease Esau. "But Esau ran to meet Jacob and embraced him; he threw his arms around his neck and kissed him. And they wept" (Genesis 33:4).

Their reunion stands as a classic example of God's urging us to settle anger with a brother or sister before offering our gifts—talents or treasures—to Him (Matthew 5:23–24). Instead, "first go and be reconciled to them; then come and offer your gift" (v. 24). Jacob obeyed God by reconciling with Esau and later setting up an altar to the Lord (Genesis 33:20). What a beautiful order: first, strive for forgiveness and reconciliation; then, at His altar, He receives us.

Against whom do you hold a
grudge or grievance? What steps
can you take to reconcile?

Dear God, when I hold on to hard feelings
against another believer, inspire me on
the way to your altar to first forgive.

Genesis 33:1–11

Jacob looked up and there was Esau, coming with his four hundred men; so he divided the children among Leah, Rachel and the two female servants. He put the female servants and their children in front, Leah and her children next, and Rachel and Joseph in the rear. He himself went on ahead and bowed down to the ground seven times as he approached his brother.

But Esau ran to meet Jacob and embraced him; he threw his arms around his neck and kissed him. And they wept. Then Esau looked up and saw the women and children. "Who are these with you?" he asked.

Jacob answered, "They are the children God has graciously given your servant."

Then the female servants and their children approached and bowed down. Next, Leah and her children came and bowed down. Last of all came Joseph and Rachel, and they too bowed down.

Esau asked, "What's the meaning of all these flocks and herds I met?"

"To find favor in your eyes, my lord," he said.

But Esau said, "I already have plenty, my brother. Keep what you have for yourself."

"No, please!" said Jacob. "If I have found favor in your eyes, accept this gift from me. For to see your face is like seeing the face of God, now that you have received me favorably. Please accept the present that was brought to you, for God has been gracious to me and I have all I need." And because Jacob insisted, Esau accepted it.

From Wisdom to Joy

*[Wisdom] will guide you
down delightful paths.*

Proverbs 3:17 NLT

The phone rang and I picked it up without delay. Calling was the oldest member of our church family—a vibrant, hardworking woman who was nearly one hundred years old. Putting the final touches on her latest book, she asked me some writing questions to help her cross the finish line. As always, however, I soon was asking her questions—about life, work, love, family.

Her many lessons from a long life sparkled with wisdom. She told me, "Pace yourself." And soon we were laughing about times she'd forgotten to do that—her wonderful stories all seasoned with true joy.

Wisdom leads to joy, the Bible teaches. "Joyful is the person who finds wisdom, the one who gains understanding" (Proverbs 3:13 NLT).

Reflecting on the matters of life, author C. S. Lewis declared that "joy is the serious business of heaven."

The path there, however, is paved with wisdom. My church friend, who lived to be 106, would agree. She walked a wise, joyful pace to the King.

⬚⬚⬚⬚⬚⬚⬚⬚⬚⬚⬚⬚⬚

What paths have you taken in trying to find joy? How can wisdom lead you to joy?

*When I might take a rocky road,
loving God, please point me back to
your path of wisdom and joy.*

Proverbs 3:13–18 NLT

Joyful is the person who finds wisdom,
    the one who gains understanding.
For wisdom is more profitable than
        silver,
    and her wages are better than gold.
Wisdom is more precious than rubies;
    nothing you desire can compare
        with her.
She offers you long life in her right
        hand,
    and riches and honor in her left.

She will guide you down delightful
        paths;
    all her ways are satisfying.
Wisdom is a tree of life to those who
        embrace her;
    happy are those who hold her
        tightly.

Remembered in Prayer

Then God remembered Rachel;
he listened to her.

Genesis 30:22

In the large African church, the pastor fell to his knees, praying to God, "Remember us!" As the pastor pleaded, the crowd responded, crying, "Remember us, Lord!" Watching this moment on YouTube, I was surprised that I shed tears too. The prayer was recorded months earlier. Yet it recalled childhood times when I heard our family's pastor make the same plea to God: "Remember us, Lord!"

Hearing that prayer as a child, I'd wrongly assumed that God sometimes forgets about us. But God is all-knowing (Psalm 147:5; 1 John 3:20), He always sees us (Psalm 33:13–15), and He loves us beyond measure (Ephesians 3:17–19).

Even more, as we see in the Hebrew word *zakar*, meaning "remember," when God "remembers" us, He acts for us. *Zakar* also means to act on a person's behalf. Thus, when God "remembered" Noah and "all the wild animals and the livestock that were with him in the ark," He then "sent a wind over the earth, and the waters receded" (Genesis 8:1). When God "remembered" barren Rachel, He "listened to her and enabled her to conceive. She became pregnant and gave birth to a son" (30:22–23).

What a great plea of trust, to ask God in prayer to remember us! He'll decide how He answers. We can pray knowing, however, that our humble request asks God to move.

※※※※※※※※※※※※

In what area of your life do you need God
to remember you? How willing are you
to pray with such intent and purpose?

*Dear heavenly Father, grow my understanding
of your remembrance of me. Then, where
I need you to act, please remember me.*

Genesis 30:1–2, 22–24

When Rachel saw that she was not bearing Jacob any children, she became jealous of her sister. So she said to Jacob, "Give me children, or I'll die!"

Jacob became angry with her and said, "Am I in the place of God, who has kept you from having children?" . . .

Then God remembered Rachel; he listened to her and enabled her to conceive. She became pregnant and gave birth to a son and said, "God has taken away my disgrace." She named him Joseph, and said, "May the LORD add to me another son."

CODA: ALL OUR HELP

We'll need a proper ending for this book, my editor said. So I set about trying to select a fitting, summarizing story for this humble collection about our helper God. Sitting at my computer, I thought of my beloved Sunday school pastor who was struck by a debilitating illness last year and the discouragement of doctors who said all was lost.

Except . . . family and friends prayed. They believed. The ill pastor prayed and believed too. Now this man—who doctors concluded would soon come to his mortal end—is back on his feet, studying his beloved Bible, praising God, and sharing the Lord and His gospel with all he sees and meets.

Or I could share about the night the heavens opened, rain fell in torrents, waters raged, viaducts flooded, bumper-to-bumper traffic across my city barely moved. But at a Denver church, folks still showed up for a little talk I was scheduled to give, and since I arrived in one piece by God's grace, we still

203

had a heart-lifting evening, talking across cultures, ethnic backgrounds, ages, and stages about the God who helps us all keep going.

Oh, there's so much any of us could say about God and His enduring, ever-present help—especially in our moments and situations of trial and trouble.

To sum up, therefore, I'll close with a battle story. A short one. A good king, Asa, had fortified the cities of Judah with fighting men who prospered their community by seeking God (2 Chronicles 14:7). Then trouble showed up. An enemy army of one million soldiers with three hundred chariots marched against Asa and Judah to take over their land (v. 9).

Taking up battle positions, Asa then

> called to the LORD his God and said, "LORD, there is no one like you to help the powerless against the mighty. Help us, LORD our God, for we rely on you, and in your name we have come against this vast army. LORD, you are our God; do not let mere mortals prevail against you." (v. 11)

Asa's was a short prayer. "Help us, LORD our God."

The Lord's response? He struck down the enemy before Asa and Judah. Then the enemy fled (v. 12). End of battle.

Jesus, in His gentle way, shows us what such battle-winning help looks like. His Love. For you. For me. For each other. As we turn to Him for help, may we each discover what His helping love does most: it draws us closer to Him to give back to the world what we all need most.

We need Him. Every hour. Our days without Him would be incomplete and empty. So He invites us to *seek Him*. Then, glory to God—He and His help are forever here.

Spread the Word
by Doing One Thing.

- Give a copy of this book as a gift.

- Share the QR code link via your social media.

- Write a review of this book on your blog, favorite bookseller's website, or at ODB.org/store.

- Recommend this book to your church, small group, or book club.

Connect with us. 🅵 🅾 🐦

Our Daily Bread Publishing
PO Box 3566, Grand Rapids, MI 49501, USA
Email: books@odb.org

Love God. Love Others.

with  Our Daily Bread.

Your gift changes lives.

Connect with us. [f] [○] [𝕐]

Our Daily Bread Publishing
PO Box 3566, Grand Rapids, MI 49501, USA
Email: books@odb.org